First published in the United Kingdom in 2022 by
Pavilion Children's Books
43 Great Ormond Street
London
WC1N 3HZ

An imprint of Pavilion Books Company Ltd

Copyright © Pavilion Books Company Ltd 2022

ISBN 978-1-84365-515-2

A CIP catalogue record for this book is available
from the British Library.

10 9 8 7 6 5 4 3 2 1

Reproduction by Rival Colour Ltd, UK
Printed by Toppan Leefung Ltd., China

This book can be ordered direct from the publisher
at www.pavilionbooks.com

FSC
www.fsc.org

MIX
Paper from
responsible sources
FSC® C104723

COOL TECHNOLOGY

JENNY JACOBY
JEM VENN

Contents

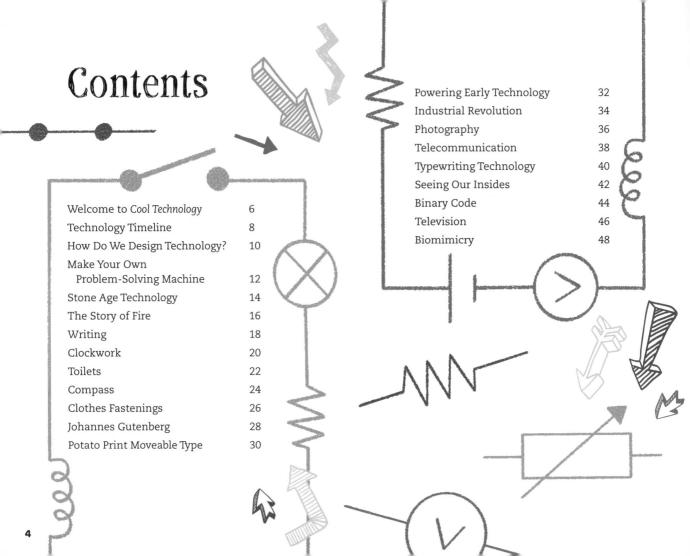

Welcome to *Cool Technology*   6

Technology Timeline   8

How Do We Design Technology?   10

Make Your Own
  Problem-Solving Machine   12

Stone Age Technology   14

The Story of Fire   16

Writing   18

Clockwork   20

Toilets   22

Compass   24

Clothes Fastenings   26

Johannes Gutenberg   28

Potato Print Moveable Type   30

Powering Early Technology   32

Industrial Revolution   34

Photography   36

Telecommunication   38

Typewriting Technology   40

Seeing Our Insides   42

Binary Code   44

Television   46

Biomimicry   48

Jean Tinguely 50

Kinetic Art 52

Annie Easley 54

Electronics 56

Plastics 58

Wendy Carlos 60

How Synthesisers Work 62

Nolan Bushnell 64

Bill Gates 66

Colour Printing 68

Mega-Ships, Mega-Ports 70

Make a Paper Boat 72

Architecture Technology 74

Shigeru Ban 76

Creative Digital Technology 78

How to Draw Pixel Art 80

Noise-Cancelling Headphones 82

GPS 84

Virtual Reality 86

Contactless Payment 88

Nanotechnology 90

Technology for All 92

Living with the Sea 94

CRISPR Gene Editing 96

Technology to Feed the World 98

Wearable Technology 100

Small-Scale Energy 102

Technology of the Future 104

Future Food 106

Living on Other Planets 108

Glossary 110

Welcome to *Cool Technology*

Nowadays it's easy to think that technology just refers to computers and software, but humans have been creating technology for millions of years.

Technology is about inventing new devices or tools that help us live our lives more easily and understand our world, and devices or tools are something everyone uses all day long. You are holding one now – this book is a device, for imparting knowledge, sparking ideas, and entertaining you. To make this book required a lot of other technology too: the computer it was written on, the tablet the illustrations were created on, the software it was designed in, and the printing press that printed and bound the pages. Not to mention the vehicles that delivered the copies to the shops and to you, the reader!

Technology can help you to be creative, and it requires creativity to design new technology. To invent a new device, you need to bring together lots of different things: knowledge of how the world works (that's the science bit), practical know-how, spotting something that could be improved with a bit of new technology, and a creative idea for how to put everything together. That's why getting out into the world, daydreaming, and observing are vital skills for anyone wanting to develop technology.

Making and using tools is something we have done from the very beginning of human history. Much of what our earliest ancestors invented is lost to the mists of time, but archaeology shows that we have always been skilled at technology and sharing our inventions so that everyone can benefit. Today we have cutting-edge technology that can help shine a light on our deepest history and tell us even more about where we came from.

As to where technology will take us in the future – not even the sky is the limit. The reality of exploring and living in space and on other planets is coming ever closer, thanks to an explosion in creative technological developments.

Bringing technology to life? Now that's definitely very cool.

'With a little imagination and a lot of patience you can make anything come to life.'

Keith Newstead

7

Technology Timeline

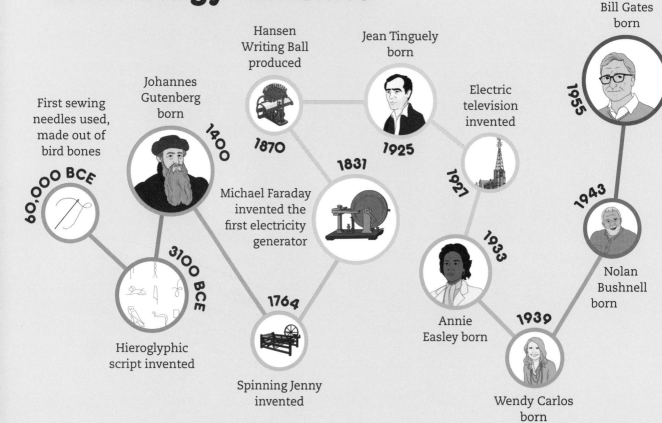

First sewing needles used, made out of bird bones
60,000 BCE

Johannes Gutenberg born
1400

Hansen Writing Ball produced
1870

Jean Tinguely born
1925

Electric television invented
1927

Bill Gates born
1955

Michael Faraday invented the first electricity generator
1831

Hieroglyphic script invented
3100 BCE

Spinning Jenny invented
1764

Annie Easley born
1933

Wendy Carlos born
1939

Nolan Bushnell born
1943

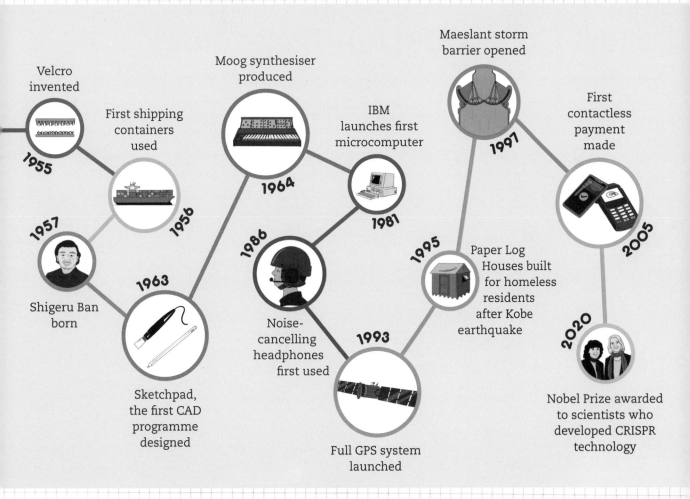

Velcro invented
1955

First shipping containers used
1956

1957
Shigeru Ban born

Moog synthesiser produced
1964

1963
Sketchpad, the first CAD programme designed

IBM launches first microcomputer
1981

1986
Noise-cancelling headphones first used

Maeslant storm barrier opened
1997

1995
Paper Log Houses built for homeless residents after Kobe earthquake

First contactless payment made
2005

2020
Nobel Prize awarded to scientists who developed CRISPR technology

1993
Full GPS system launched

How Do We Design Technology?

Everybody can be a brilliant inventor and design technology. You don't have to have a degree in engineering to have a great idea and start designing it (though you might need some expert information to make the final design). There are three main steps to designing an invention, and everyone already has these skills. Here is how an inventor puts them to use...

Coming up with ideas

Inventors look at the world around them and daydream. They pick an interesting topic and consider how technology could address it. Inventors spend a lot of time thinking closely about the topic, but at this point they don't worry about how realistic their invention is. The idea is key: only when an idea has been thought of can it be invented.

Inspiring inventor questions to ask yourself:

What interests me?
What annoys me?
What is a problem that I could solve?
What do I love to do that isn't possible for everyone else to do?

Experimentation

Next, the inventor starts playing. They sketch out their idea or use materials to build a rough 3D version of it. They might start out roughly and get more and more precise with each sketch and model. By trying things out in 2D or 3D they can begin to see problems they would need to solve to bring the technology to life. They list those problems and use them as things to work on in the next stage. Building a model is called prototyping – inventors might make several prototypes at different stages of a project.

Collaboration

The next stage is sharing their ideas and prototype with a team. The best teams are made up of people with different skills and knowledge so that they can help to solve the list of problems uncovered by the prototyping. The team members may also spark new ideas about improving the technology. Working as a team, there will need to be a few more rounds of experimentation and collaboration before the idea can be brought to life as a real technology.

Make Your Own Problem-Solving Machine

Have a go at designing your own problem-solving machine using the design process. How far to go? That's up to you – the only limit is your imagination!

You Will Need

- Paper and pencil

- Junk modelling materials such as: toilet roll tubes, yoghurt pots, jars, string, buttons, tapes, lids, old toys, scrap fabric, googly eyes, stones, sticks, sand, leaves, moss, pine cones

- Tools such as: sticky tape, glue, safety pins

Remember:
Don't worry about making your sketch perfect! Any kind of sketch is useful. The word 'sketch' implies that it isn't perfect.

Let's get started

1. Think about a problem you would like to solve. Look back at page 10 to see how inventors come up with ideas.

2. Think freely to come up with some different ideas for how to solve the problem. List everything – even if at first it seems ridiculous!

3. Choose one of your ideas to develop. You might want to sketch it out first. What items could you use from your collection to help build the model?

4. Start constructing your machine. Pay attention as you go to anything that you think could be improved – even if you don't have the right materials with you now, note down what could help or be made better.

5. When you have made your model you might want to stop there – and keep the model as a reminder to always pay attention to your ideas, and see how far you can take them.

6. Or – don't stop there! With your list of ways to improve the model, see who you can find to help you go further with improving your model and maybe developing it even more.

Steps to success

- Allow yourself to be creative and silly. The more ideas the better – even if they seem impossible! You never know what might spark something useful.

- Prototyping is the best way to learn. Even if it's not perfect, you'll learn new skills and might come up with ideas for next time.

Stone Age Technology

Ninety-nine percent of human history happened during the Stone Age, so it makes sense that some of our most transformative technology developed in this era. Most but not all of the tools in the Stone Age were made from stone – the clue's in the name! Intelligence allowed humans to turn stone to tools, and in turn allowed humans to change their lives and environment forever.

Stone tools

By striking flint and other types of rock in particular patterns with another hard rock, all sorts of useful stone tools were made.

Hand axes were used for chopping meat, breaking open animal bones and cutting wood.

Blades were cut straight and much sharper than hand axes. Their sharp edges were used for carving antler and bone into other useful tools.

Scrapers, with their sharp, flat edges, were used to scrape flesh and hair from animal skin so it could be turned into leather or furs. They needed to be less sharp than blades to scrape without cutting into the skin.

Microliths were small, very sharp points of stone snapped off from a blade, which could be used as arrow points.

Sewing needle

Once the needle and thread were invented in the late Stone Age, people could make clothes that fitted them – useful for the harsh climates of the Ice Age. Sewing needles were shaped from animal bone and threaded with plant fibre.

Cool facts

- It was during the Stone Age around 130,000 to 90,000 years ago that humans spread out from Africa to all continents (apart from Antarctica).
- Humans all over the world developed different tools to live successfully in each environment.
- Even tattooing dates back to the Stone Age!

Rope

Stone Age rope, called cordage, was made from strong plant fibres such as nettles. First the stems were stripped of leaves, and then crushed by hand. With the outer layers taken off, the inner layer was left to dry out before being twisted or plaited into rope. The cordage was used for carrying firewood, making baskets and building shelters.

The Story of Fire

Long before people knew how to make fire they were aware of the power it held, as they watched wildfires burn through forests and scare away other animals. So when humans worked out the technology to control fire, they suddenly had a huge advantage over all other animals.

Uses of fire

Fires can keep you warm, which helped people live in the cold regions of the world during the Ice Age. They also provide light, which was useful when people moved further from the equator, where there is less daylight in the winter.

With a campfire at night, people could not only keep warm but were also protected from the large predators of the Stone Age – animals don't like to come too close to a fire.

The biggest difference that comes from controlling fire, though, is cooking food. Cooking kills off bacteria and makes food easier to digest. When people started cooking food, they were less likely to get ill and could stay healthier and live longer. All this extra energy available from food may have allowed our brains to grow bigger too, and develop even more technology to help ourselves.

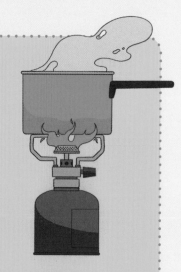

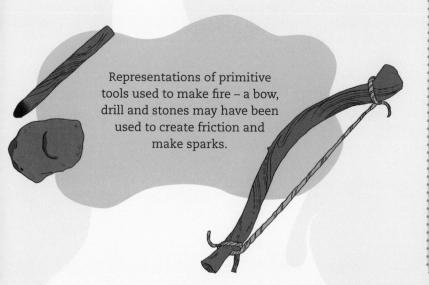

Representations of primitive tools used to make fire – a bow, drill and stones may have been used to create friction and make sparks.

In the home today
Although today we can have our own fire at the flick of a switch or scratch of a matchstick, we still reap all the same benefits from fire that our Stone Age ancestors did: light, warmth, and safety. Even if we don't have fire directly in our homes, it still helps fuel many electrical power stations.

Writing

One technological invention from ancient history that makes this book possible is writing. Invented separately by at least four groups across the world, it is impossible to imagine the world without writing as a part of communication – and different groups have invented completely different systems for writing.

What is writing?

What makes writing different from drawing or other communication markings is that it represents spoken language. When someone reads writing, they hear the words spoken as language inside their mind. In this way, writing records language so it can be shared among more people than could originally hear spoken word, and it lasts much longer.

Writing needs to be done on a surface, whether that's physically in clay, carved into stone or ink on paper, or digitally on modern computers and tablets.

Before writing

There were many other symbolic written forms before proper writing was developed – such as records of the number of animals belonging to a person, or the passing of time.

Stories were passed across great distances and through generations by storytelling – to entertain, educate, and bring people together. Ballads, myths, and long poems were spread through word of mouth. Some were very long and difficult to memorise.

The invention of writing

The first true writing dates back to 3,400–3,100 BCE in two places: Mesopotamia and Egypt. Cuneiform, the written language in Mesopotamia, used pictograms (small, stylised pictures) to represent a word. As time went on, these pictures simplified into symbols. Hieroglyphics, invented in Ancient Egypt, was based on pictures or glyphs that represented a thing or action, and a sound or sounds.

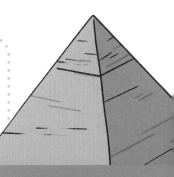

The benefit of writing

When epic poems began to be written down, the Ancient Greek philosopher Socrates thought that it was a bad idea because people would become forgetful if they didn't exercise their memories. But today we can be happy these ancient stories were written down so that we can enjoy them too. Once recorded, stories usually become fixed; when they are told orally details are more likely to change and evolve. Writing is more reliable for recording and remembering facts.

Different systems

LOGOGRAPHIC: Each character represents a whole word – 'logogram' means 'word-picture'. Today, written Chinese, Japanese and Korean are all logographic.

ALPHABET: Each letter represents a sound that can be put together to represent words, using consonants and vowels. The main alphabets in Europe are Latin, Cyrillic and Greek.

ABJAD: This script comprises of consonants only. Vowel sounds can be added with accents. Written Arabic, Urdu, Punjabi, Farsi and Hebrew are abjad scripts used today.

ABUGIDA: These scripts are made up of consonant and vowel units. Abugidas are used in many written languages including Thai, Ethiopian and Tibetan.

Clockwork

Clockwork is an ancient technology that allows mechanical energy to power a machine through a series of wheels, gears, handles, teeth and other carefully shaped pieces. Clockwork often includes a way of storing energy and slowly releasing it over time, to power the mechanism at a steady rate. Still used today in toys, timers, watches and clocks, this technology is so useful and popular because it doesn't require electricity.

How does it work?
Clockwork devices can be very simple or incredibly complex. Most clockwork devices contain four parts:
- A key (or crown) for winding up and adding energy to the mechanism
- A spiral spring for storing the energy
- Gears to control the pace and power that the energy is released at
- A mechanism to do useful work with the energy, such as clock hands travelling around a clock face

Music box
One of the simplest ways to understand clockwork is through a music box. Turning the handle turns a toothed wheel which is attached to a cylinder marked with small dots of metal. As the cylinder turns, the dots catch on thin strips of metal which make different musical notes as they ping. The arrangement of the dots controls the timing of each note to play a piece of music.

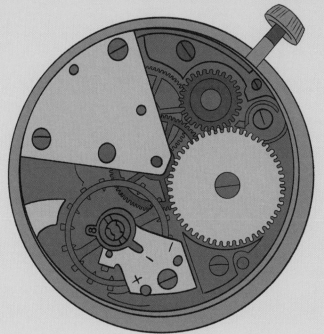

Clocks and timers

The right combination of wheels, gears and springs allows hands to move around a clock face at the right speed. Each minute, after completing one journey around the clock face, the second hand causes the minute hand to move forward one notch. The minute hand is controlled by its own gear that has sixty notches in it, so that after sixty minutes, it returns to the top of the clock face and causes the hour hand to move forward one notch.

When was clockwork invented?

We don't know! Legends talk of clockwork wonders as far back as the fifth century BCE, but the oldest clockwork mechanism ever found is the Antikythera mechanism, which was made in the first century BCE in Ancient Greece. It predicted eclipses and the positions of the stars, and was so complex that the technology must have been developing in Ancient Greece for a long time to reach that level. Europeans lost the knowledge of making clockwork until after the Crusades in the Middle Ages, when they brought back the know-how from the Islamic world.

Toilets

If using a flushable toilet every day seems unremarkable, you are one of the world's lucky people. One in four people in the world today do not have a toilet of their own to use. That's two billion people!

Why are decent toilets important?

Toilets need to be somewhere clean, safe, and private, where waste can be removed or made safe – if human waste is left untreated, it can spread germs into water sources and food. The Romans were some of the first people to have public toilets, made of a wooden board with holes in that ran across a trench sewer system. But these latrines were not very clean and so didn't stop some of the deadly diseases that waste can spread, such as diarrhoea and cholera.

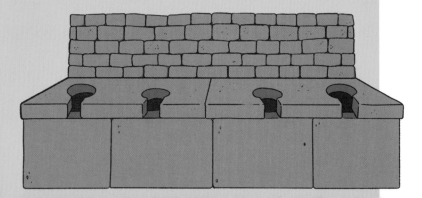

What a waste!

Ever since humans have lived in big settlements, there has been the problem of what to do with dirty waste water. However, in the nineteenth century when populations in cities boomed, it was often emptied into rivers that people also used for drinking water, causing big health problems.

Modern waste treatment

Luckily sewer systems have developed since then. For most of us, waste travels in a sewer pipe from our home to a sewage treatment plant. There, it can take as little as four hours for sewage water to be clean enough to return to rivers.

How does it work?

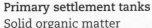

Inlet works
Screens remove any large solid lumps such as stones, wood, or rags that have accidentally got into the system

Primary settlement tanks
Solid organic matter is removed as it filters through rows of tanks

Processing
All the sludge removed is then dried out into 'cakes' which can be burned for fuel or used as fertiliser

Testing
Resulting treated water is left to settle before careful testing to make sure it's safe to return to local rivers or the sea

Secondary treatment tanks
Sewage is mixed with billions of bacteria and pumped with air to break down any remaining harmful materials and germs

Can toilets be cool?
Public toilets in Japan can be high-tech – the seat can disinfect itself, and you can have background music (to entertain you or drown out any sounds!) and a water jet to clean you afterwards. Pretty cool!

Alternatives to flush toilets
The flush is common now, but composting toilets are older pieces of tech that are still safe and environmentally friendly. They are useful in rural areas without sewers or running water. Pits of waste are covered with ash or sawdust to remove smells and decontaminate waste to make compost for fertilising crops.

Compass

The compass was invented more than 2,000 years ago in China. This ancient piece of technology was made by harnessing natural magnetic fields and using them as a tool to navigate unfamiliar places.

How does it work?

Compasses work by magnetic force. All magnets have a north pole and a south pole, and opposite poles attract each other while like poles repel each other. When a compass needle is able to swing freely, it orientates itself so it points north. Compasses come in a case marked with the points of the compass, which can be moved so that the mark for 'north' aligns with the direction the compass is pointing. The user can then work out which way they need to travel, and keep track of the way they are going.

How was it invented?

If you play with two magnetic rocks you'll soon see how one pair of sides attracts and the other pair repels. A breakthrough moment in the invention came when people realised that the Earth has a magnetic field. If a magnet is thin enough and able to move by itself, it will always point north.

The first magnets were made from lodestone, which is naturally magnetic. To make it free to spin, the stones were shaped to be able to float in water. One Chinese design was the 'south-pointing spoon', which was shaped to move freely on a dry surface.

What was its impact?

From around 200 BCE, early compasses in China were used for a sort of fortune telling rather than navigation. It wasn't until the eleventh century that armed forces used the compass for navigation.

Before compasses were invented, people used landmarks and the position of the stars in the sky as guides for the direction they should travel. But on a cloudy night at sea, there's no way to be sure which way is which. The compass enabled people to travel further, which increased sailing, trade and exploration.

Cool facts

- Compasses weren't used in Europe or the Islamic world until 1190.

- 'True North' – the top of the Earth's axis – isn't actually the same as 'Magnetic North' – the place compass needles always point to. Magnetic North is about 1,000 miles south of True North, in Canada.

- Magnetic North moves around the Earth over time. Over the last hundred years, it has moved around 600 miles towards Siberia.

- A magnetic rock found in Mesoamerica might also have been used as a compass, which would predate the Chinese invention by a thousand years, but nobody has proved its use yet.

Clothes Fastenings

Some things you use every day are so small that you don't think about them until they break. There are many ways to fasten your clothes to keep them on you and feeling comfortable, and they work best when you don't even notice them. Sewing was invented in the Stone Age, but to take clothes on and off as well as shape them comfortably involves extra fasteners. Here are the stories behind some of the ways you do up your clothes and shoes.

Brooches

Simple clothing of the Bronze Age in Europe involved a loose tunic with a hole to slip over the head. This was shaped like a keyhole so when the tunic was on, the slit part was fixed together with a brooch to keep out the cold.

Laces

From around the twelfth century, people in Europe started to lace their clothes to bring the edges of garments together more comfortably. Holes for the laces would be carefully cut and sewn around to strengthen them – sometimes a small metal ring was used to make it very robust. Because laces can adapt to the body's shape, they were a popular way of fastening clothes right up to the start of the twentieth century, with women's corsets using laces to exaggerate the shape of the body.

Buttons

Decorative beads were popular on outfits for centuries before people realised they could fasten clothes. Then buttons became very popular in Medieval Europe, as rich people chose to wear snug-fitting clothes. While they are still an important part of clothing today we tend to use fewer buttons than people in the past, who felt the more the better!

Zips

Zips became popular in clothing from the 1930s, but they were invented years earlier – it took a long time to perfect the design and for everyone to accept this new form of fastener. But once they did, people never looked back!

In the 1890s, an American travelling salesman called Whitcomb Judson invented a version of a zip that used a series of hook-and-eye clasps unfastened by a slider – but it never worked very well. The company who took on Judson's invention changed the clasps for a simpler method we see in zips today: rows of teeth that interlock with 'scoops' fitting together like spoons.

Zips were used for soldier's money belts in the First World War, and then in the 1920s on rubber overshoes. The more zips were used on clothes, the more popular they became, and today you can find them on clothes everywhere.

Velcro

The technology behind this easy to fasten and open fabric was inspired by nature. In 1941, Swiss engineer George de Mestral was walking in the mountains when he realised that burrs had stuck to his trousers and to his dog's fur. Under a microscope, he could see the burrs had tiny hook shapes that attach easily to loops of fabric – and dog hair!

After years of research, George created two strips of fabric – one of tiny hooks and one of tiny loops – and eventually realised that nylon was a more resilient fabric to use than cotton. He patented Velcro in 1955 – the name is a mix of 'velvet' and 'crochet'.

Velcro is now used in all sorts of clothing, shoes, games, on some medical equipment, and even on NASA spacecraft to stop items floating about in space.

Timeline
Brooches *Bronze Age*
Laces *12th century*
Buttons *13th century*
Zips *1930s*
Velcro *1955*

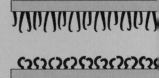

27

Johannes Gutenberg
Printing for the people

Johannes Gutenberg was born in Germany in the fifteenth century and his work helped to bring in a revolution in literacy and education across Europe that shifted the medieval era into the Renaissance. His invention: the moveable type printing press.

> Like a new star it shall scatter the darkness of ignorance, and cause light heretofore unknown to shine amongst men.
>
> Johannes Gutenberg

The first books

In medieval Europe books were beautiful, hand-crafted tomes that were copied out painstakingly slowly by hand. They were therefore very expensive and owned only by the rich upper classes. In China, Japan and Korea, books were printed using blocks – whole pages were carved into wooden blocks, which were then covered in ink and pressed onto paper.

A revolution in printing

Johannes was a craftsman and inventor who designed a wooden printing press that could print efficiently – about 250 copies per hour. But the most revolutionary part of his invention is moveable type. He used his metalworking skills to cast whole upper- and lower-case alphabets in different sizes, as well as a range of punctuation out of various metals, such as lead and tin.

These characters could be arranged into a frame to create a 'page' of type and once all the copies of the page were printed, the letters could be reused. Much quicker and easier than carving a whole new block of wood!

Books for all

By printing more copies more quickly, without losing any quality, books could be sold much more cheaply. Now, people in all levels of society had access to books, and therefore to information and ideas. This explosion in information sharing led to revolutions in scientific, political, religious and philosophical thinking, and the world was changed forever.

A masterpiece

Gutenberg's masterpiece of printing was the '42-line Bible', completed around 1455. Approximately 180 copies were printed, but today only around forty copies still exist.

Not the first moveable type

Moveable type had been invented decades before Gutenberg in China and Korea. But after Gutenberg's invention, the idea took off much more rapidly in Europe than in Asia because European script is made up of a small alphabet of letters, compared to the thousands of individual characters in written Chinese. Whole books could be created out of a much smaller set of characters, which kept the process quick and easy, and therefore cheap.

Potato Print Moveable Type

Johannes Gutenberg revolutionised printing with his metal moveable type. Don't have his metalworking skills? You can do (almost) the same with just a potato and a knife, some ink and paper – carefully carving each character (letter forms or numbers).

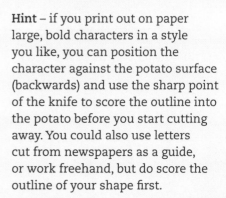

You Will Need

- Some potatoes (how many depends on how many letters you want to make)
- A sharp knife – take care when cutting and ask for help if you need it
- Kitchen roll
- Poster paints
- Paper
- Printouts of characters for inspiration

1. Cut a potato in half. The flat inside surfaces will hold a carved character each. Remember – you'll need to carve each character as a mirror image for it to print the right way round.

2. **Hint** – if you print out on paper large, bold characters in a style you like, you can position the character against the potato surface (backwards) and use the sharp point of the knife to score the outline into the potato before you start cutting away. You could also use letters cut from newspapers as a guide, or work freehand, but do score the outline of your shape first.

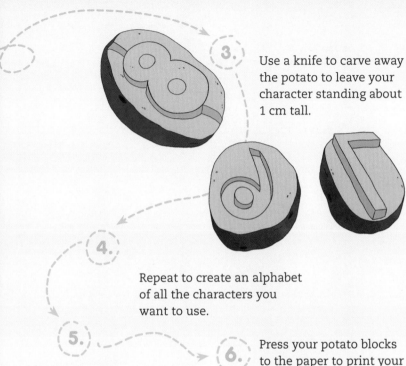

3. Use a knife to carve away the potato to leave your character standing about 1 cm tall.

4. Repeat to create an alphabet of all the characters you want to use.

5. Blot each potato character dry with kitchen roll before you carefully apply paint to the surface. The drier the potato, the easier it is for your paint to stick to the potato block.

6. Press your potato blocks to the paper to print your message!

123456
789

Steps to success

- You can use any sort of potato but consider using ones a good size for your hand to comfortably hold.
- If you have large potatoes you may be able to cut them into more pieces and get more characters from each one. Make sure you leave enough potato to hold easily.
- You can choose whether you want each character to be positive (where you cut away parts of the potato that aren't the character) or negative (where you cut away the character form and leave the negative space).

Powering Early Technology

Back before we learned to generate and control electricity, people used power from different natural sources to power technology, and designed the technology specially to fit the power source.

People power

Incredible feats of engineering have been achieved using the strength of people pulling together as a team. Although we aren't sure how prehistoric monuments such as the pyramids of Ancient Egypt or Stonehenge in England were made, whatever technological tools enabled these huge rocks to be moved would have been powered by the strength of many people working together.

On a more everyday scale, farmers used a scythe and their own strength to cut grass or crops, as far back as 5,000 BCE. It is an efficient technology that is still in use today in some parts of Europe and Asia.

Horse power

As long as they were trained and cared for, horses were a useful way of powering lots of technology. Pulling ploughs and harvesting machinery, horses often performed the heaviest farm work. They also powered much of the early industrialised world, including pulling canal boats delivering coal to factories and driving buses and coaches in cities and the countryside. Horses had one big drawback though: the amount of poo they produced which needed cleaning up!

Wind

The earliest wind-powered technology was probably sail boats. Later, the idea of capturing wind power in sails was transferred to powering windmills and windpumps, which are used to move water out of low-lying land such as in the Netherlands, so the land can be farmed and lived on.

Water

River water moving downstream has a huge amount of power. A waterwheel turned by rushing water can in turn power machinery attached to the axle of a wheel. The first watermill dates back to the third century BCE in Ancient Greece. The machinery powered a millstone to grind grain to flour, but waterwheels also powered all sorts of technology, from cutting equipment in sawmills to rollers in paper mills and blast furnaces.

Rivers are usually dependable energy sources but in times of drought or flood their power can still be unpredictable – and often dangerous.

Industrial Revolution

Beginning in Britain in the 1700s, a series of tech breakthroughs brought on the Industrial Revolution, transforming the world forever. It changed the way goods were made, from being handcrafted by experts in small workshops, to large, noisy factories where each worker repeated individual parts of the process. This change sped up the rate goods could be made, making things cheaper and easier to buy.

Technology took over skills that people had trained for years to perfect, and angered many who lost livelihoods when their skills were no longer needed. In some cases these new technologies were built and used in secret to avoid upsetting workers.

Spinning machines

When the 'flying shuttle' machine was invented in 1733, weavers could produce more cloth more quickly. This caused a new problem: linen and cotton thread couldn't be made quickly enough to keep up with the weavers. In 1764 James Hargreaves invented the spinning jenny which could spin eight times more cotton yarn than a person. By bringing the production of fabric from workshops into factories, over time improvements to the technology enabled even more thread to be spun at a time.

Steam engine

The invention of the steam engine allowed energy to be turned on when needed – rather than relying on wind, water, or limited manpower. It produced enough power to move all the heavy steel machinery in the factories popping up across Britain. These engines work by burning coal to produce steam, which builds up so much pressure that it can easily move pistons to power factory machinery.

In 1814, steam engine technology was adapted by George Stephenson to create locomotive trains, allowing goods and people to be moved faster than ever seen in history. At first the locomotive was used to move coal from mines to factories, so that they could keep working faster and faster.

Electric generator

Michael Faraday was a self-taught scientist whose research into electricity and magnetism led to his invention in 1831 of the Faraday Disc: the first electricity generator. While scientists had experimented with electricity for decades, this was the first time anyone found a way to create and control an electric current at will. Ever since, people have come up with countless ways to use electricity, and our lives are dependent on it for cooking, heating, light, and much more.

Photography

Ever since the Renaissance, artists had been trying to capture reality in painting. All that changed in the nineteenth century when a new technology appeared that was better at recording a moment of reality than any artist: photography. It changed the way we see and record the world forever.

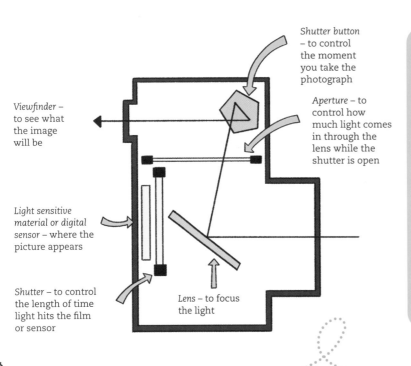

Shutter button – to control the moment you take the photograph

Aperture – to control how much light comes in through the lens while the shutter is open

Viewfinder – to see what the image will be

Light sensitive material or digital sensor – where the picture appears

Shutter – to control the length of time light hits the film or sensor

Lens – to focus the light

Ingredients for a photograph

Several people were involved in the invention of photography, each building on the others' discoveries, but by the early 1800s the ingredients had been discovered for using a camera to produce a photograph. These have been improved upon ever since, but whether using film or digital cameras, all photographs are taken by controlling the amount of light allowed to pass through a lens that focuses it onto a light-sensitive material.

Printing

If a photograph is taken on a film camera, it creates a 'negative' image on the film. When the negatives are developed and fixed, they can be used to print 'positive' images on light-sensitive photographic paper. Light shines through the negatives so that dark areas on the negative block light, leaving light areas on the photo. Digital camera images can easily be printed by a digital printer (see page 68).

The camera never lies

Although the image taken by a camera reflects exactly what it sees, images can be manipulated to trick others or show an altered version of reality. Software for 'retouching' photos can correct or completely change colours, remove blemishes and reshape objects. Images can even be combined so a group of people can look like they were together even if they never actually met each other.

Image manipulation is not new. In 1917 two young girls took photographs of themselves with fairies in their garden – known as the Cottingley Fairies – which looked so realistic that many people believed the photos were proof fairies existed. The girls didn't admit until 1983 that they had used cut-out drawings in their photos!

Manipulating photographs can be fun, but it can pose ethical problems, especially if someone claims a false image is true, or misleads public opinion.

Telecommunication

For thousands of years, humans have used technology to communicate when they're too far away to talk or shout. Communication technology continues to develop rapidly, becoming easier, cheaper, and quicker. Over the last century, the main ways of communicating have changed from letters in the post and phone calls to homes, to text messages, video calls, and social media.

Early telecommunication

Long-distance messages could be sent from anywhere high enough to be seen or heard a great distance away. These were often alarms to warn that an enemy was approaching. Beacon towers along the Great Wall of China used smoke signals in daylight, and fires in the dark. When the Spanish Armada was approaching England in 1588, beacons of fire were lit along the coast, quickly sending a visual alarm.

Sound is also useful, and in cultures living in forested areas where it's hard to see long-distance, people sent signals through loud rhythmic drumbeats.

Telephone wires

Telephones are made up of three parts:

- A metal or plastic speaker that vibrates to reproduce the sound waves
- A microphone that translates sound vibrations into electrical signals
- A switch or keypad to dial the phone directly to the person you are calling

The telephone sends electrical signals down copper wires, and the phone company connects the caller's phone wires directly to the recipient's for the call.

Radio waves

Mobile phones aren't connected to wires, so the phone translates sound into electrical signals, and sends them out as radio waves. These are electromagnetic wiggles in a pattern representing the sound. Radio waves are caught by a cell tower and sent on to the recipient's phone, which turns the electrical signals back into sound. Each cell tower covers a certain area, so the signals might travel far between several cell towers, or even by satellite.

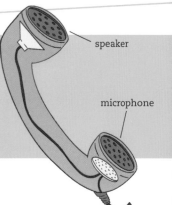

speaker

microphone

Modern telecommunication

Since the 1870s we have had technology to help us speak or send sound – and much more – across long distances.

Fibreoptics

All kinds of information are sent around the world at the speed of light through fibreoptic cables. First, devices code information into data to send through the cables as pulses of light. The light travels to the receiving device which decodes the info and displays it or recreates the sound.

Glass fibreoptic cables are about the width of a human hair, and this small size enables light to travel so far because of a phenomenon called Total Internal Reflection. When the light hits the side of the cable, it doesn't scatter but bounces off the side at the same angle. In this way, the pulses of light bounce down the cable at the speed of light.

To help keep the information going over long distances without losing strength, amplifiers boost the signal at different stages along the way. Fibreoptic cables are cheaper, more powerful and can travel further than copper wires.

Typewriting Technology

Over the last 150 years, we have become more dependent on technology for writing. Typewriters can be quicker to use and their output easier to read than handwriting. They were partly developed to help blind people to write, as once you have learned the position of the letters on the keyboard you can type anything. Typewriters became popular in offices long before homes: the writing is longer lasting, and it's harder to erase or counterfeit so is great for public records.

Typewriters

Typewriters were invented at least 52 separate times. The first was in 1575 in Italy, but the first commercial typewriter was the Hansen Writing Ball, first produced in 1870. Each letter was on a piston that punched ink directly onto the paper. The letters were positioned so the most frequently used were near your fastest fingers – this made the machine much quicker than writing by hand.

Typewriters were much more successful in countries with alphabet writing systems rather than logographic, such as Chinese and Japanese, because fewer keys are needed.

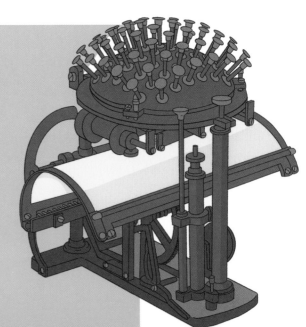

Word processors

As soon as ink hits paper on a typewriter, it is hard to edit the words. Electronic word processors help this by allowing typed words to be checked on a screen before they are printed onto the paper.

Computers

As personal computers became more popular in households through the 1980s and 90s, people abandoned big pieces of hardware built purely for typing. However, computers still looked a little like typewriters, keeping the usefully designed QWERTY keyboard. It was no longer just trained secretaries who were able to type quickly, and accuracy became less important as word processing software on computers made it easier than ever to correct typos and format documents before being printed out or shared on the internet.

Texting

Smart phones often still use the QWERTY layout, but rather than using ten fingers on a keyboard, people have become super-fast at writing with one finger or two thumbs. The more a person types, the better their phone becomes at learning and predicting what word will come next. This makes it even quicker to tap out a message to a friend or a blog post. Whole books have even been typed out on phone keyboards!

Seeing our Insides

In the past, the only way scientists could see inside us was by dissecting dead bodies. This was helpful for learning about anatomy and how the body fits together – but it was limited in how it could help people while they were alive. In the 1890s a new discovery changed the way we view our bodies forever.

X-rays

- Scientist Wilhelm Röntgen discovered X-rays in 1895 while experimenting with cathode rays (glass tubes containing a gas and an electrical current). When he held his hand between the tube and a chemically treated screen, it produced an image of his bones. It wasn't long until the medical world adopted Röntgen's technology.

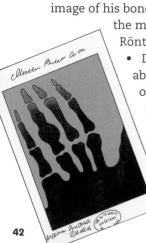

  - Different body parts absorb different amounts of X-rays. Bones absorb more than skin, so they show as whiter where more rays have been absorbed, and skin as darker where more rays make it to the screen.

- Being exposed to X-rays can be dangerous. Today, X-rays are still used in hospitals to look at bones and check organs, but they are weaker and many safety precautions are used.

Ultrasound

Ultrasound technology can look at organs, muscles, joints, and babies before they are born, because it is safer than using X-rays. A probe sends sound waves and 'listens' for echoes as the sound waves bounce off tissues in the body. A computer translates the echoes into an image on a monitor.

Ultrasound scans can take place through the skin or even from a flexible tube with a light sent into the body, to see what is happening where food goes.

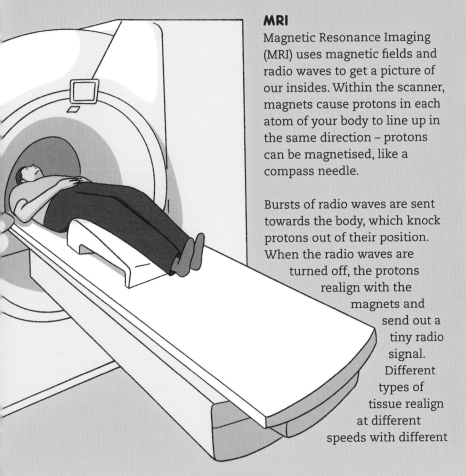

MRI

Magnetic Resonance Imaging (MRI) uses magnetic fields and radio waves to get a picture of our insides. Within the scanner, magnets cause protons in each atom of your body to line up in the same direction – protons can be magnetised, like a compass needle.

Bursts of radio waves are sent towards the body, which knock protons out of their position. When the radio waves are turned off, the protons realign with the magnets and send out a tiny radio signal. Different types of tissue realign at different speeds with different signals. These are translated by the computer into an image of inside the body. Having these MRI scans is safe because magnetic fields and radio waves don't damage the body.

Cool facts

- X-rays were given their name because the scientist who discovered them had no idea what they were!

- X-rays are actually invisible electromagnetic waves with short wavelength – they have a lot of energy but don't travel great distances.

- Marie Curie helped to develop 'radiological cars' with portable X-ray machines so soldiers at the front in the First World War could be quickly treated by doctors.

- X-rays were even used in shoe shops until the 1950s to help ensure shoes fitted well.

Binary Code

All digital technology involves binary code. In fact, when we talk about 'digital' technology, it is all created using binary code. While we count in continuous numbers, computers only understand two digits: O and 1. All the information we create, transmit and use on computers has to be translated into binary code of O and 1... and then translated back to us in the language we understand!

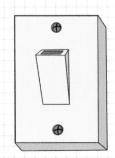

What does binary mean?
'Binary' means being made up of two things: two states or ways of being. A switch, for example, can be off or on; it cannot be partially on. Compare that to a human: people can be awake ('on'), asleep ('off'), or any level of sleepiness between fully awake or asleep. This ability to be somewhere between completely on or off is called *analogue*, and it's the alternative to *digital* or binary states, where you can only be one of two things.

How does it work?
Computers use binary code because a 1 can represent a pulse of electricity or light or information, while a 0 represents no information, or 'off'. Pulses sent in the right pattern can easily be translated by the computer back into analogue information for us to understand.

Computers and other technology can break down almost any piece of information into tiny pieces and give it a value in binary code.

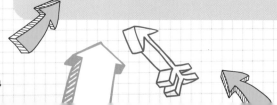

What is binary code?

We are used to counting in sets of ten – this is called 'denary' or 'decimal'. Binary is a number system that only uses 0 or 1. Both systems rely on place value – the position a digit is in gives it its value. Rather than going up in tens, binary place values double at each position. For example, the number 111 has different values in the two systems, and this is how they are worked out:

Denary place values ->	100	10	1
Number 111 ->	1	1	1
Binary place values ->	4	2	1

To work out the value of 111 in the two systems we have to do three little sums where we multiply the value (1) by the place value it is in:

Number	1	1	1
Denary sums	100 x 1 = 100	10 x 1 = 10	1 x 1 = 1
Binary sums	4 x 1 = 4	2 x 1 = 2	1 x 1 = 1

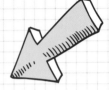
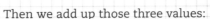

Then we add up those three values:

Denary sums	100 + 10 + 1	= 111
Binary sums	4 + 2 + 1	= 7

In the denary system, 111 has a value of 111. In the binary system, 111 has a value of 7.

In denary, the number three thousand, four hundred and sixty-one looks like this: 3,461. In binary code, the same number is represented like this: 10100101.

That might be hard for people to understand – but for technology, it is much easier to process, store and transmit a series of zeros and ones than to hold a large number like 3,461 in its memory.

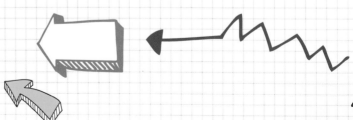

Television

Television technology involves three inventions: how to change sounds and images to code, how to transmit that code from the broadcaster to televisions, and how to display that code as moving images and sounds that we sit down to enjoy every day on our televisions.

The BBC transmission mast in North London is one of the oldest in the world, and is considered the birthplace of television.

How was it invented?

People began experimenting with ways to transmit sounds and pictures in the nineteenth century. Lots of different inventions laid the path to the invention of television as we know it – and several inventors got there at about the same time, in the 1920s, using different methods.

How does it work?
Encoding

Moving pictures and sounds are encoded into electrical impulses. The video camera sections up an image into dots called 'pixels' that it captures as electronic signals, called the video signal. The microphone captures the accompanying sound as the audio signal, and both together are called the TV signal. One image is called a 'frame' and the camera records twenty-four frames per second, each broken down into pixels.

Transmitting

TV signals were originally sent as radio waves but these can struggle to reach mountainous or remote areas. In the 1940s, cable TV emerged, sending signals via underground cables. Now, TV signals can be bounced up to a satellite and then back to any TV globally, or transmitted over the internet.

Decoding and displaying

Old cathode ray TVs decode video signals into pulses of electrons, and shoot them onto the screen in the right pattern. The screen reacts, displaying the beams as pixels to make up the picture. Today, TVs are more commonly LCD (Liquid Crystal Display) or plasma flatscreens. The electrical pulses of the video signal move through the liquid crystal screen, which lets through light in the right pattern to make the images.

Whatever the type of screen, we see twenty-four frames per second, which is fast enough that our brains combine the images to make it seem to us that they are actually moving.

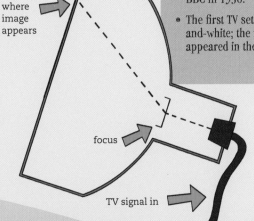

TV screen where image appears

focus

TV signal in

Biomimicry

What nature has invented through evolution has sparked ideas for people making technology. This is called biomimicry – because it is mimicking something from the natural world. Lots of today's designs use techniques from nature to produce technology more in tune with the natural world, or to be more eco-friendly. People take inspiration from nature's forms, processes, and ecosystems.

Catseye

The name for these reflective dots that help night-time drivers see road and lane edges comes from the technology's inspiration. In 1933, Percy Shaw was driving home on a dark, foggy night on winding country lanes in England. In the darkness, Percy suddenly saw two glowing points of light – the eyes of a cat on a fence, reflecting the light from his car. Percy's invention was patented in 1934 and used all over the world.

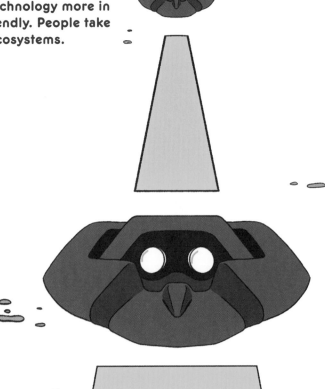

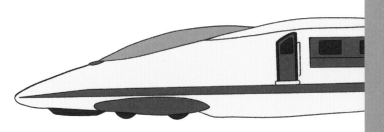

Kingfisher bullet train

Japan's Shinkansen trains are known as bullet trains as they travel so fast – up to 150–200mph. They had a problem though: every time they sped through tunnels, they pushed the air out in one big burst, making a huge boom sound that disturbed not just the passengers, but people and animals near the tunnel.

Engineer Eiji Nakatsu, who also enjoyed bird watching, noticed how a kingfisher's beak allowed it to dive quickly and easily into water. He realised that bullet trains moving into tunnel air faced the same issue as kingfishers dipping into water. He mimicked the kingfisher's long, pointed shape in a redesign of the bullet train's nose. The redesigned trains are faster, quieter, and more powerful with 30% less air resistance – just like a kingfisher!

Termite air conditioning

Termites control temperatures inside their termite mounds by changing how air flows inside it, and how much the sun hits it. The architects of the Eastgate Centre in Harare, Zimbabwe, took inspiration from termites and built ledges over the windows to provide shade and send hot air out of the roof. Fresh air is cooled in the basement before travelling around the building. Steel columns help to support vines, so the building encourages nature and acts like an ecosystem. The Centre uses 35% less energy than buildings with traditional air conditioning!

Jean Tinguely
The art of kinetic technology

Born in 1925, this Swiss artist was interested in how art should respond to the increasingly technological world of his time – including the technological warfare of the Second World War. His response was motor-powered sculptures made from metals, motors, and everyday items from rubber, string and cardboard to bicycle wheels and enamel bathtubs.

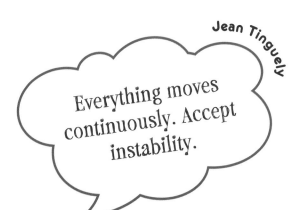

Jean Tinguely

Everything moves continuously. Accept instability.

Meta-mechanical art

Jean used ideas from technology and clockwork to create moving sculptures. Where abstract artists before him had painted static art, he used motors to turn abstract compositions into moving works of art.

His sculptures were designed to not work perfectly – their unpredictable and unreliable movements were the opposite of how the industrial world around him worked. While modern technology worked with mathematical precision, his sculptures took a different approach, to show the beauty in chance movements, random-ness, and things always changing.

Is it art?

Many of Jean's artworks were interactive – the audience could move sculptures by pressing a button, or even walk inside them. His art invited the audience to see how things worked by showing the technology that made them go – all the mechanics were on show rather than neatly hidden away. Audiences could see the cause and effect inside the machine – such as the turn of a cog causing a handle to flap – which made a change from complicated everyday technology they used without understanding how it worked. This made the works playful and engaging, and very different from the static paintings and sculptures that filled art galleries at the time.

Self-destructive art

Some of Jean's artworks were designed to explode and destroy themselves. These spectacular explosions were events – some of the first performance art – so that the art existed only for one moment. He filmed sculptures exploding so that afterwards the film was all that was left. Jean didn't believe that all art should be collectable and kept forever in museums. His art showed that sometimes technology ends in destruction.

Kinetic Art

Make your own piece of kinetic art with this homemade pendulum painting contraption.

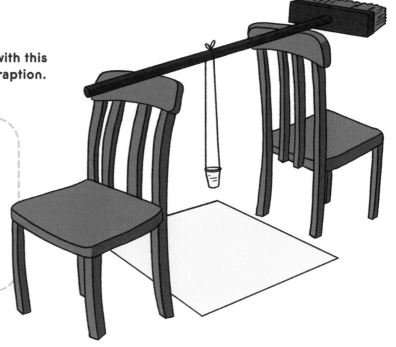

You Will Need

- Two chairs the same size
- A broom handle or long straight piece of wood
- String
- Paper cup
- Sharp pencil
- Hole punch
- Washable paint
- Water
- Large piece of paper
- Protective tablecloth or newspaper

Let's Get Started

1. Lay the wipeable tablecloth or newspaper over the floor, then place the large paper on top.

2. Create the stand for the pendulum by placing two chairs back to back, about 1 metre apart, either side of the paper. Balance the broom handle across the backs of the chairs.

3. Mark two places directly opposite each other near the top of the cup. Use the hole punch to make holes here.

4. Use the sharp pencil to punch a hole in the centre of the cup's bottom.

5. Thread the string through both holes at the top of the cup and tie the string so the cup hangs from the broom handle, about 12 cm from the floor.

6. Mix one part paint with two parts water so it is runny.

7. When you are ready to go hold a finger over the hole in the bottom of the cup and pour in the paint. Hold the cup up to one side, let go and watch the cup swing!

8. Try out different colours of paint and swirling the cup in different patterns.

Steps to success

- Try experimenting with using slightly different height chairs so the broom is wonky and seeing how that affects the painting.
- The length of string you use to attach the cup depends on the chairs you have used.

- You can use a piece of tape over the hole in the bottom of the cup to keep the paint in until you are ready to go.
- If the paint is coming out in splotches rather than a swirl, try adding more water to make it thinner.

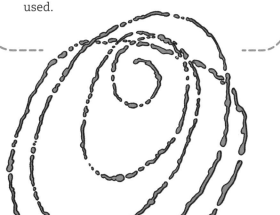

Annie Easley
Pioneering rocket scientist

Annie Easley was one of the first African-Americans to work as a computer scientist at NASA. She encouraged women and students from minorities to study and choose STEM subjects as careers – and she helped launch the Cassini probe that landed on Saturn.

Don't give up on it. Just stick with it.

Annie Easley

Alabama

Annie was born in Alabama at a time when African-Americans had limited access to education or careers, and Black and white children were educated at separate schools. Although her environment was against her, Annie's mother encouraged her that she could be anything she wanted if she worked hard enough. Annie left Alabama to study pharmacy at university, though she only studied for two years before her life took a different course.

When Annie registered to vote in Alabama she discovered that African-Americans had to pass a literacy test and then pay a fee to be allowed to vote. Because of her university education she had no trouble, but she decided to work helping others to overcome those restrictions.

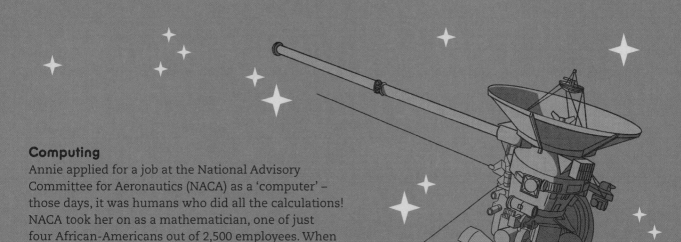

Computing

Annie applied for a job at the National Advisory Committee for Aeronautics (NACA) as a 'computer' – those days, it was humans who did all the calculations! NACA took her on as a mathematician, one of just four African-Americans out of 2,500 employees. When actual computers arrived, Annie learned to code and became a programmer.

Into space

NACA became NASA and Annie worked on many different projects over her thirty-four-year career there. She developed code to analyse different power sources, and to support the *Centaur* rocket.

Centaur was made to launch heavy loads such as satellites and probes into space, and it sent up Surveyor 1, the first American space probe to land on the Moon, as well as the Cassini probe which landed on Saturn.

She persisted

While she worked for NASA Annie continued her education and in 1977 she graduated from Cleveland State University with a degree in mathematics. Annie retired from NASA in 1989 after 34 years' service.

Electronics

A lot of technology requires electricity to make it go. Electronics is the study of working with electricity to make it do useful things. Once you know the basics, you can use a few simple principles to build all kinds of useful technology.

In the loop

From the simplest electronics to the most complicated, all electronic devices require three things to work:

- A power source (a battery or being plugged in to the mains supply)
- An electrical device (such as a lightbulb, a fan or a buzzer)
- Wires to connect the two in a complete, closed circuit

Circuits can include lots of other useful components, such as a switch or motor, as long as the wires connect in to one side and out the other so that the circuit remains whole and unbroken.

We use symbols in diagrams of electronic circuits to show what components are being used and how they are connected to each other. Here are some of the most common:

Lamp

Switch

Battery

Insulation and conduction

Materials that electricity flows through are called **conductors**. Metals are excellent conductors because the electrons in metals are free to flow through a circuit. Most wires are made from copper. Unfortunately, electricity can also flow through water and living things – that is why electricity can be dangerous and you should never let an electrical device come close to water.

Materials that resist electricity are called **insulators**. Wires in your home will have a copper core, where the electricity flows, covered by a plastic insulator that keeps the wire safe to handle. Wood, glass and rubber are also good insulators.

Electricity flow

Electricity works because the battery powers the electrons in the metal wires so they flow around the circuit, from the negative end to the positive end – as long as the circuit is complete. If the circuit breaks then the electricity cannot flow, so it stops and will not power the device.

To control the flow, switches break and reconnect the circuit so we can turn off a light, for example, when we aren't using it.

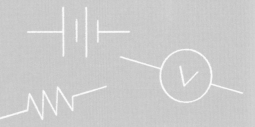

Plastics

When plastic was invented around a hundred years ago it was hailed as a wonder material. There are many different types, but plastics are all non-natural materials that can be moulded into shape and set as rigid or elastic. After the Second World War, plastic use boomed. Although we know plastic can be problematic, it has so many uses that it is hard to give it up – could it play a part in creating a more sustainable world?

How is it made?
Chemicals extracted from coal, oil, cotton, water, and air are made to react together in a process called *polymerisation*. This is where the molecules form into new strings of long molecules called *polymers*. The different chemicals that make up the polymers give different characteristics to the resulting plastic.

Some plastics, called *thermoplastics,* can be heated up to soften and be reshaped, but others, called *thermosets*, cannot be reshaped once they have set the first time. That means they can't easily be recycled.

Why was it invented?
Natural plastic-like products were valued before any synthetic plastic was invented. Rubber gum from trees was used to make cloth water resistant, and varnish came from a resin made by the lac bug.

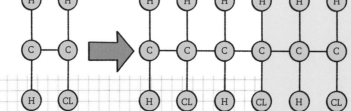

What's the catch?

Plastic never goes away. It just gets smaller and smaller as it breaks down, and we now know the dangers that come with microplastics entering the ecosystem. As plastics break down in rivers and oceans, they can be ingested by fish and other sea life. When we eat these fish, we also eat the plastic and over time that can build up in our bodies. We don't yet know the extent of the problems this can cause.

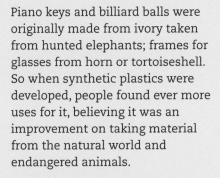

Piano keys and billiard balls were originally made from ivory taken from hunted elephants; frames for glasses from horn or tortoiseshell. So when synthetic plastics were developed, people found ever more uses for it, believing it was an improvement on taking material from the natural world and endangered animals.

More uses for plastic keep being found – today, plastic on clothes makes them much longer lasting and more comfortable to wear in extreme conditions.

Plastic today

Plastic is popular because it's so useful. With a densely populated world, plastic helps with food distribution, energy production, and water conservation. Because it's so durable, we need to make sure we only use it when it is the best material for the job, and can be reused for as long as possible.

What's the alternative?

Eliminating single-use plastic is a good idea, and there are many alternatives in use already, such as:

- compostable drinks cups
- beeswax cotton wraps
- washable nappies
- stainless steel straws
- bamboo disposable cutlery

People are also recycling discarded plastic into useful things, from fishing nets to bags to flip-flops.

Wendy Carlos
Electronic music pioneer

Wendy brought together her two talents of music and computing to develop and popularise the budding electronic music scene in the 1960s and 70s. Celebrated by *Keyboard* magazine for her 'subtlety and delicacy of detail', she brought the technology of electronic music into something the public loved, through her best-selling albums and movie soundtracks.

You should take advantage of what skills and talents you're born with but there's no way around learning some composition, arranging, performing, timbres, plus all the tech stuff.

Wendy Carlos

Musical roots

Growing up in a musical household, Wendy started piano lessons when she was six, and at age ten she composed her first piece: 'A Trio for Clarinet, Accordion and Piano'. It wasn't just music that inspired her, though, and aged fourteen she built a computer to present at a local science fair, which won her a scholarship. At Brown University, Wendy studied music and physics, then a masters degree in music composition at Columbia University.

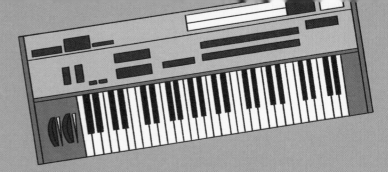

The Moog Synthesiser
In the mid-1960s Wendy met Robert Moog, who was developing the Moog synthesiser. Synthesisers back then were huge – filling a room – so not very practical, and only found in laboratories. They were played using punchcards, but the Moog used a keyboard which was more appealing for musicians. Wendy gave advice to Robert to improve his synthesiser, as he was an engineering expert but she had more experience as a composer and performer. She owned a Moog synthesiser herself from 1966, which she used to make music for advertisements.

The synthesiser sound
In 1968, Wendy released *Switched-On Bach*, an album of classical music played on a Moog synthesiser. Nobody expected the album to be quite so popular: it was the first classical music album to sell a million copies, and one of the first electronic albums to reach the charts. Recording it had required a lot of patience as only one note could be played at a time, and it was difficult to keep the machine in tune. But Wendy's dedication to her craft paid off.

Promoting electronic music
Wendy's clear and friendly way of talking about her work makes her an advocate for electronic music technology, keen to share her knowledge and enthusiasm. But she also knows that 'art comes from creative people doing a job well' – just because the technology is available to all doesn't mean everybody can suddenly become a talented composer unless they put in the work.

How Synthesisers Work

'Synthesise' means to put together, and a synthesiser is a piece of music technology that creates sound by putting together electronic tones. This can artificially reproduce sounds of traditional instruments as well as new, electronic sounds. When synthesisers were first invented, they were large pieces of hardware but today they can be part of virtual studio technology in a Digital Audio Workstation. Software is cheaper and offers a lot more possibilities than hardware, though this means it can also be complex to use.

Input

First, you need to input a note. That is usually done by pressing a key on the keyboard.

Oscillator

The sound from the keyboard is created electronically by an oscillator. To oscillate is to move in a steady rhythm, and a synthesiser oscillator creates sound waves at a constant, steady pitch.

Envelopes and filters

These are dials on the synthesiser that adjust parts of the sound's volume, shape or tone. Amplitude (or volume) envelopes include:
Attack – how quickly the loudest part of the note occurs.
Decay – how quickly the sound signal reaches the level set by the sustain.
Sustain – the lower volume level the sound stays at while it's being played.
Release – how quickly the sound takes to die away.

Synthesising

The sound waves can be put together to create a sound ('additive synthesis') or filtered to remove frequencies from the sound waves ('subtractive synthesis'). By changing the way the sounds are put together and manipulated, one keyboard note can change its sound completely – perhaps the sound of a plucked string or that of a trumpet! Electric keyboards today have a synthesiser inside them to do just that, at the touch of a button.

Sound waves

A *sine* wave makes a simple, slightly muffled, flute-like sound.

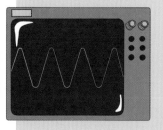

A *triangular* wave accentuates the higher frequencies, so makes a brighter, cleaner sound than a sine wave but less harsh than a sawtooth wave.

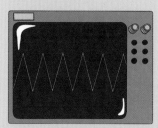

A *sawtooth* wave sounds harsh and buzzy.

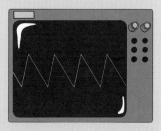

White noise looks like a scribble of a wave, and sounds like heavy rain or the roar of a very busy road.

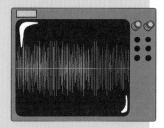

Timeline

1897 – Thaddeus Cahill's Dynamophone: an early electric organ

1928 – Léon Theremin's theremin: a contactless synthesiser with electronic oscillators

1956 – RCA Electronic Music Synthesiser Mark I: a huge piece of hardware combining electronic sounds with a sequencer

1964 – Moog synthesiser: the first commercial synthesiser

1970 – Minimoog: the first affordable, portable synthesiser

1970s – digital synthesisers

1983 – Yamaha DX7: popular in 80s pop music

Nolan Bushnell
The father of video games

When computers were developed, it didn't take long to find ways to make them fun as well as helpful. Nolan Bushnell is one of the entrepreneurs who brought together computer technology, a nose for business, and the psychology of game playing, to explode the popularity of computer games through the company he co-founded, Atari.

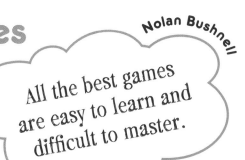

Nolan Bushnell

All the best games are easy to learn and difficult to master.

The business of games

Nolan studied electrical engineering and business at university in the 1960s, where he enjoyed playing an early computer game called *Spacewar!* that was only found in university computer labs. He also had a job at a local theme park, which got him interested in arcade games – particularly what drew someone to pay to play a game, and the combination of skill and luck that helped them to win. He realised he could make a business bringing computer games more cheaply to more people.

Where it started

In 1972 Nolan and Ted Dabney founded Atari, named after a move in one of Nolan's favourite board games – the name means 'about to win'. One of Atari's first games was the enormously popular *Pong* – a simple game where two players each control a bat that can only move up and down, to hit a ball back and forth. As the game goes on the ball travels faster, making the game harder. Because the technology was so limited compared to computer games today, Nolan focused on making Atari's games extremely playable and responsive.

From *Pong* to pizza

Atari started off making games for video arcades, and then in 1977 launched the Atari 2600, a video game console for people to play at home. It came with two joysticks, paddle controllers and a game called *Combat*. People could buy other game cartridges as extras, including *Pac-Man* and *Space Invaders,* the two most popular games of the time.

Nolan had dreamed of launching a chain of pizza parlours filled with arcade games, and in 1977 he launched the Chuck E. Cheese Pizza Time Theatre chain restaurants, where families could eat pizza and play video games. This was the first time video games were available to children and a family audience.

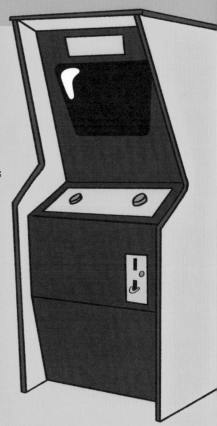

Bill Gates
Microcomputer revolutionary

Bill Gates is one of the founders of the Microsoft Corporation, the world's largest personal computer software company, and has frequently been named the richest person in the world.

The advance of technology is based on making it fit in so you don't really even notice it, so it's a part of everyday life.

Childhood
Bill wrote his first software program when he was thirteen – a noughts-and-crosses game you could play against the computer. At high school he helped to computerise the system for scheduling classes, and he founded a company called Traf-o-Data that made systems for counting traffic, which they sold to local governments.

Birth of the microcomputer

Until the early 1970s computers were large, expensive systems. The microcomputer was a breakthrough in computer hardware because all the processing could be done on one circuit rather than many large circuit boards. Computers could then become smaller and cheaper. This happened back when Bill Gates was at Harvard University, studying computer science.

Birth of Microsoft

It was the release of one of the first microcomputers, the Altair 8800, that gave Bill an idea. Still at university, Bill and his school friend Paul Allen developed software to run on the platform and demonstrated it to MITS, the company that made the Altair 8800. MITS agreed to distribute the software known as Altair BASIC. So, in 1975 Bill dropped out of Harvard and set up the company Microsoft with Paul.

From software to billionaire

In 1981, IBM launched their first microcomputer, called the IBM PC, using Microsoft's MS-DOS operating system. This not only gave the world the term 'PC', which took over from 'microcomputer' and is still in use today, but gave Microsoft a prestige that made them the world's leading software company. By 1986 Bill was worth a billion dollars. While leading the company, he continued writing code through the 1980s.

Bill stepped down from Microsoft to concentrate on the Bill and Melinda Gates Foundation, a charity tackling global problems.

Colour Printing

Although it wasn't until the 1990s that newspapers started printing colour images, the technology for printing in full colour dates back to the 1900s. Today we print with digital presses as well as on presses using printing plates, but both techniques use just four colour inks to create all the colours you see in a printed picture.

CMYK

Printed colour images are made from four basic colours: **Cyan** (light blue), **Magenta** (bright pink), **Yellow**, and **Key** (black).

Printing in layers of tiny dots tricks your brain into seeing the image in a bigger range of colours. Different strengths of cyan and magenta on top of each other gives reds and purples; cyan and yellow gives greens and blues, and so on. The range of colours that CMYK can produce is called the gamut.

How does it work?

Visible light is made from all the colours of the rainbow. When we see yellow it's because the object absorbs all the colours except for yellow, which it reflects back at us. By adding more colours in different mixes, the colours are taking away different parts of the light and reflecting less of the visible light to us. This is why the CMYK printing process is called **subtractive** – because it's taking away light.

Four-colour separation

Today, a computer can quickly break an image down into CMYK, but originally a camera would have taken separate photos using individual CMYK filters. The negatives from the camera were used to make plates for printing from.

Printing

As the paper rolls through the printing press, first the cyan (C) is printed. Then the magenta (M) on top, then the yellow (Y) on top of that. Lastly, the black layer (K) is applied, which adds in the last bits of detail and depth to the picture.

Impressionism

The idea for creating coloured images out of dots of a few simple colours came after the Impressionist painters developed pointillism paintings, where what looks like a bunch of dots up close looks like a realistic painting from a distance.

Up close

If you look closely at a colour picture printed in a newspaper you might notice the picture is made up of 'rosettes' of coloured dots. Up close, it's hard to make out what the picture is of, but when you move the picture slowly away you'll see the dots start to make sense as a colourful image.

Mega-Ships, Mega-Ports

We have been sailing and using ports for thousands of years, and as shipping and docking technology has evolved we have been able to sail bigger ships containing more cargo across the world. Many everyday items will have spent time on a container ship, from your food to your phone to your books. A few strategically placed ports – Rotterdam, Singapore, Los Angeles – have become so big and busy we call them mega-ports. So how does shipping work at today's mega scale?

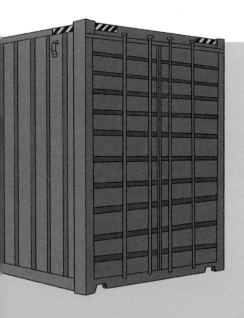

Organising

The biggest technological development in the efficiency of global shipping came with using containers. These are standard-sized large metal containers that shipping companies sell space in to send goods overseas. Before containers, goods came in all sorts of sizes and were jumbled up in the ships. Using standard containers makes it easy to organise and fill ship space for a voyage. There can be thousands on a ship at a time!

Before any cargo comes near a ship, planners work out where in the ship each container will be placed. This is partly to ensure the weight is distributed safely, and partly to know where each company's cargo is located. This information is needed at loading and unloading.

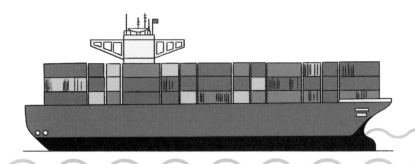

Docking

It can take hours just to bring a mega-ship alongside the port for docking because to move carefully they must move slowly. Small tug boats can push and pull a container ship into place – sometimes working as a team of four to one giant ship.

Mooring

Robot-powered magnetic plates and mechanical levers can hold a ship in place in port – but most ships are still secured by one of shipping's oldest tools: ropes. This old technology is so useful because the ropes can slacken and tighten as the tides come and go, allowing the boat to float comfortably as conditions change.

Loading...

At the port, each container is identified by its own ID number, so huge cranes can lift it into its pre-chosen position onboard. Containers are stacked up in the ship's hold as high as 40 metres. Long vertical guides ensure the containers are held straight and safely in place. Some containers are stored on the deck and secured with strong metal rods, tightened manually by dock workers.

...and unloading

Huge cranes remove the containers in order so each container ends up where it is meant to go. The containers are moved by machines to a storage yard before they go out for delivery. This process can be automated using programmed computer software to direct and drive the containers around the port, and store them in the most efficient way for when each container will be collected.

Make a Paper Boat

One sheet of paper and a few careful folds and you can set a ship sailing. You might not be able to fit much cargo on it, though...

You Will Need

- One sheet of A4 paper

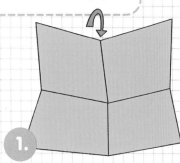

1.

Fold the paper in half twice and then unfold it so that you can see the paper divided into four. Now fold the top of the paper down to the bottom.

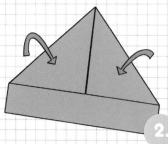

2.

With the folded edge at the top, fold down the top right corner to meet the middle fold line. Repeat with the top left corner.

3.

Fold the bottom right corner up to meet the horizontal edge. Repeat with the bottom left corner.

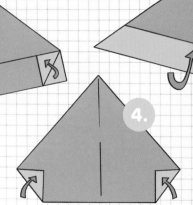

4.

Flip the paper over and repeat fold this fold on the bottom corners on the other side.

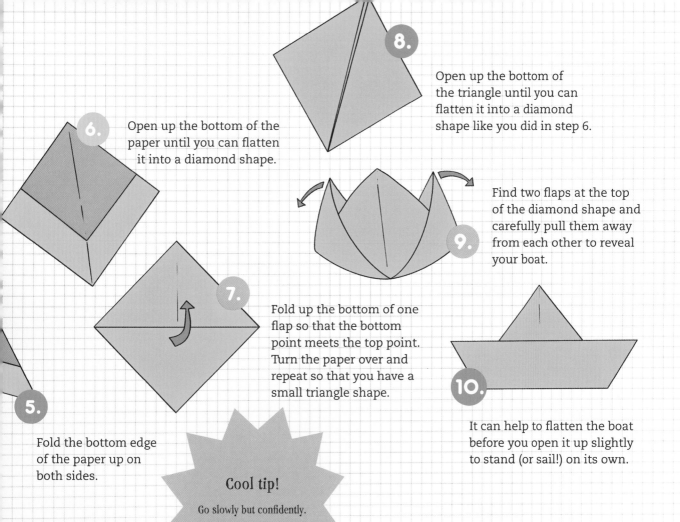

8. Open up the bottom of the triangle until you can flatten it into a diamond shape like you did in step 6.

6. Open up the bottom of the paper until you can flatten it into a diamond shape.

9. Find two flaps at the top of the diamond shape and carefully pull them away from each other to reveal your boat.

7. Fold up the bottom of one flap so that the bottom point meets the top point. Turn the paper over and repeat so that you have a small triangle shape.

5. Fold the bottom edge of the paper up on both sides.

10. It can help to flatten the boat before you open it up slightly to stand (or sail!) on its own.

Cool tip!

Go slowly but confidently.

Architecture Technology

Architects use their creative brilliance to design buildings that are useful, beautiful and awe-inspiring. But to take a new design from a drawing on the page or screen to a fully functional building requires technological know-how.

What does it involve?

When an architect designs a building, a whole team gets involved to design a range of systems that help the building to work. These could include electricity, fresh water, wastewater, heating, ventilation, security, waterproofing, and fireproofing. It can also involve using new technology to make a building work more cleverly or in a more environmentally friendly way. The more technology that is developed, the more opportunities architects have to incorporate useful features in their buildings.

Fire safety

Fire has always been a risk for buildings and after any devastating fire, technology steps in to help make it less likely. After the Great Fire of London in 1666, all new buildings were required to have window sills for the first time, as this small bit of stone protected the upper floors if a fire started on the floor below.

Today we know the importance of being able to contain any fire in as small an area as possible, not allowing it to spread. Buildings now have strict fireproofing standards, including using fire doors and fire-resistant materials, smoke alarms to alert people, and sprinklers – like indoor rain to help put out the fire before it can spread.

Transparent toilets

Glass coated with liquid crystal that turns from see-through to opaque at the flick of a switch has been used to create beautiful public toilets that solve two common problems. People worry before entering a public loo that there might be someone already in there, and whether it is clean enough to use. When the toilets are empty, people can see in to check, but when they lock the door the glass turns opaque for some privacy!

3D printed homes

Using mud and clay as the material in a large 3D printer, small shelters can be printed almost anywhere. The process is quick and the building material is cheap and eco-friendly. In the future we could solve emergency housing needs this way – and when they're no longer needed, the buildings can return to the earth. Maybe one day we will even build permanent homes with a 3D printer.

Why is architecture technology cool?

Some technology is discovered almost by accident, and it takes an architect's creativity to find ways to use it. Other technology is developed because there is a demand for it. This makes architectural technology a playground for creativity while solving important problems in everyone's daily life.

Shigeru Ban
Good on paper

Japanese architect Shigeru Ban is known for creating buildings and homes from very low-tech materials such as paper and cardboard – showing that sometimes common materials can be given new, important uses through creativity and technological spark. In addition, Shigeru strives to care for humanity and the environment in his work.

Paper technology

Shigeru discovered the joy of making architectural models from paper when he was at school. When he was studying architecture at university in California, he used paper because it was cheap and plentiful. But it wasn't until he finished his training and was back in Japan, putting together an architecture exhibition, that he started to consider paper and cardboard as building materials. Shigeru wanted to display 'bentwood' designs, but it was too expensive to use wood so instead he used paper tubes to create a similar sense of an undulating wall.

Shigeru felt sure that paper could become more useful – but the technology wasn't out there yet, ready for him to use. Shigeru had to prove paper was usable himself by fireproofing and waterproofing the tubes, and even building his own weekend home out of cardboard tubes to convince authorities that it could work as a viable building material.

Disaster relief

Many of Shigeru's buildings respond to disasters, providing much needed shelter. Seeing the plight of Rwandan refugees in 1994 pushed Shigeru towards making shelters out of recycled paper tubes, an idea that the UN took up and that inspired Shigeru's future work.

The 1995 earthquake in Kobe, Japan, destroyed much of the city and left many residents homeless. Shigeru designed Paper Log Houses as temporary homes that are cheap and fully recyclable. The design has been adapted after earthquakes in Turkey and India, using found local materials and even rubble. In Turkey the tubes were filled with shredded wastepaper to give greater insulation.

In 2011, an earthquake destroyed the cathedral in Christchurch, New Zealand. While the city decides on a suitable replacement, Shigeru's temporary Cardboard Cathedral was built less than two years later, and will last for up to fifty years.

Creative Digital Technology

Since the 1980s, software on personal computers has given a huge range of tools to creative artists, designers and innovators who previously worked with their hands to create 2D and 3D artworks, advertisements and entertainment. But the story of Computer Aided Design (CAD) and Manufacturing (CAM) goes back much further...

The first CAD

As with lots of tech, CAD sprung from work for the military. In the early 1950s Douglas T. Ross was a university researcher working on military radar technology when he developed the first CAD systems. The first true CAD software was developed in the 1960s. Called Sketchpad, the user interacted with the computer by using a light pen to draw on the computer monitor. It wasn't too different from using your finger to draw on a smartphone but there were many years in between those technologies!

Cool art

Today, illustrators and artists often use software apps for tablets that mimic the natural feel of drawing, but result in a digital artwork that can be tweaked and manipulated. This can be quicker and less messy for artists, and the artwork can then be easily shared and used in other software, such as typesetting for book design.

Graphic design

Into the 1990s, printed materials were designed by pasting each part of the page onto special paper marked up with the margins and lines to help the designer lay everything out precisely. If anything needed to be corrected at this point, it was possible but took time and was expensive. When ready, the pages would be photographed by a special camera to create a negative film that was used to make the printing plate for the printing press.

Since 'desktop publishing' software was introduced, all the parts of a page layout are easily moved about and any mistakes can be corrected quickly before going to print.

Of course, not everything is printed now – entertainment and information can exist entirely in digital form and changes can be made instantly.

Why is it cool?
In the same way personal computers brought technology out of laboratories and into people's homes, creative digital software has brought a world of creative possibilities into people's hands – and they are being made even simpler to interact with on a smartphone.

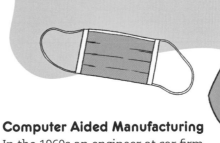

Computer Aided Manufacturing
In the 1960s an engineer at car firm Renault created software to bring together the drawing machine and surface design with the machines that create car models.

Fast foward to today, and with the right software and a personal 3D printer, you can manufacture physical items in your own home! At the beginning of the COVID-19 pandemic in 2020, eight-year-old Londoner Nahla-Rose Bartlett-Vanderpuye used a 3D printer to make protective equipment that hospitals were desperate for.

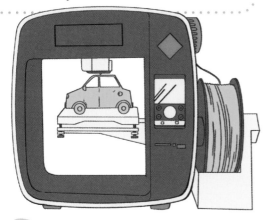

How to Draw Pixel Art

Get the computer art look on a piece of paper – and enjoy the peace of colouring in. The fun of this is that you can start with a hand-drawn look and end up with something that looks like it belongs on an 8-bit computer screen.

You Will Need

- Graph paper
- Pencil
- Felt-tip pens or coloured pencils in different colours
- Eraser

2. Take the first colour pencil and fill in a single square wherever there is a pencil line – even if it only goes through a small part of it.

Let's Get Started

1. Using your pencil lightly, draw your picture on the graph paper. Include outlines of any detail or where your colours will change.

3. After you've coloured in the boxes along the lines of your drawing, make sure you fill in the boxes between those lines too.

4. Repeat this with the other colours you're using until your drawing is finished!

Steps to success
- Each box should be completely filled in or left empty – no box should be part filled.
- Colour in the boxes as neatly as you can.
- You can print out graph paper if you don't have any. The more squares per centimetre the sharper your picture will seem – but it can look more fun if you use larger squares.
- Try outlining the different colour sections of your drawing with a black felt-tip. Does it make your art look clearer, or more pixellated?

Noise-Cancelling Headphones

Headphones that not only deliver sound to your ears but also cancel out other noises were invented in the early 1980s, but they were only available to the military at first. Now, anyone can buy a set to enjoy listening to the sounds they choose while drowning out background hubbub.

Why were they designed?

The headphones were first used by the US Air Force to help pilots cope with the noisy work of flying fighter planes. Hearing loss was the second-most common reason for pilots to retire early, so the Air Force needed to find a way to help its staff. People who work in noisy environments often use earplugs – but this stops them from hearing useful noises too. In very noisy workplaces, such as in aircraft, helicopters, tanks and around heavy machinery, the deep, throbbing background noises aren't cut out by earplugs anyway.

Noise-cancelling headphones allow the sounds you have chosen to listen to – perhaps music, or ground control talking to a pilot – to be heard clearly in your ears with all the background noise taken out.

How do they work?

American company Bose is known for making speakers and other hardware that produces sound – but they developed noise-cancelling headphones by using something called *antisound*.

Antisound is the opposite of sound. Sound travels in waves, so where the sound wave has a peak, the antisound has a trough, and vice versa. When the sound and antisound waves meet, they cancel each other out.

In noise-cancelling headphones, there is a microphone that picks up unwanted background sounds and then an electronic circuit quickly analyses and produces an opposite sound. The antisound is fed into the speaker to cancel out its opposite sound, so that the wearer hears their chosen sounds and none of the background sounds.

The headphones are insulated so that no other noise can leak into or out of the wearer's ears without being processed by the circuit.

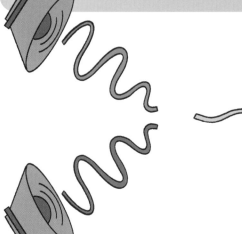

Future noise-cancelling technology

Using the same principle of antisound to cancel out unwanted noise, researchers in Singapore are developing a way of cancelling traffic noises that come in through open windows. In hot weather, opening the window for a breeze can be unpleasant due to noisy traffic – but with well-positioned noise-cancelling speakers, this problem could soon be cancelled too.

GPS

GPS stands for 'Global Positioning System' and it is the way our smartphones and GPS devices know where we are in the world. The system can give an accurate location to within 7.8 metres, 95% of the time.

How was it designed?

The US military created the GPS system, and Russia developed a similar system called GLONASS. Both are used for free by people around the world with the right devices, though the US Armed Forces have got an even more accurate version for their own use only.

The US Navy started using satellites to help submarines navigate, back in the 1960s. Early computer programmers developed code to process information from satellites to work out their exact location. This helped to model the precise shape of the Earth, including mountains, seas, and any changes brought about by tides.

Then the US Department of Defence adopted this satellite navigation system in the 1970s, and the full system launched in 1993.

How does it work?

There is a network of more than 30 satellites in orbit around Earth that are dedicated to the GPS system. The satellites travel around the Earth two times a day. Each satellite contains an extremely accurate clock, and continually broadcasts the time in its signals to Earth.

Devices on Earth receive information from at least four different satellites about their location and the time the message was sent. A device can then use this information to calculate the difference in time between sending and receiving the messages, to work out exactly where in the world it is, including altitude (how high above sea level it is).

The devices are pre-programmed with map information so that it can use GPS to show the user their location on the map.

Other uses

GPS satellites are also useful in monitoring large natural phenomena such as tsunamis, volcanoes and earthquakes, and can be useful to give us an early warning of something big happening.

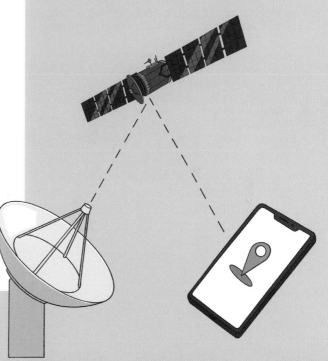

Virtual Reality

Virtual reality (VR) is a way of experiencing a computer-generated environment in 3D so that it feels like you are really there – it's not reality but it aims to be as immersive as possible. You can see and hear things in the VR world but you can't touch, smell, or taste anything virtually... yet!

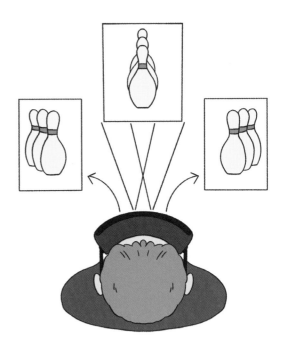

How does it work?

A virtual reality experience involves both hardware and software. The hardware is a headset for viewing and hearing the VR, and the software plugs into it, programmed with the particular VR environment. So you only need one piece of hardware to enter any number of VR worlds.

A VR headset is **stereoscopic** – meaning that there are two scenes shown next to each other and as your brain blends the two images together, the image you experience is in 3D. This is just like how we see the real world. What really helps this 3D experience to become immersive is that the headset can respond to where the viewer is looking.

Sensors track the viewer's head and eye movements and adjust what part of the scene it shows.

When the viewer moves, the VR responds by letting the person 'walk' through the environment. Some VR sets include hand controllers so that the person can interact with objects in the VR.

What's it used for?

VR is popular in gaming – entering a VR environment can be a lot of fun, and feel like an escape from normal life while you complete tasks or quests in a game. But VR is also used in training to give people experience and practice in situationsthat could be rare or dangerous in real life – such as doctors learning surgical procedures or pilots learning to fly.

The future of VR

VR can bring people together virtually, without needing to actually travel. Since the COVID-19 pandemic, more people have become interested in experiencing things outside the home without actually going out, and in socialising while being socially distanced. VR can even be a way to watch a film with the feeling of it being at the cinema – and with friends in other places experiencing the same VR cinema at the same time, you can get together with your friends virtually.

Contactless Payment

A contactless payment means tapping your contactless card or device over a reader that can accept the payment. This way you can pay for things without handling cash or physically tapping in a PIN code. During the COVID-19 pandemic, as many tried to avoid contact with other people and objects as much as possible, contactless payments took off. By 2021 in the UK, one in three card payments was made using a contactless card.

How does it work?

Contactless payment cards contain a chip that emits radio waves called radio-frequency identification (RFID). When the card comes close to a contactless reader, an antenna in the card communicates with the reader securely over RFID to process the payment. The information shared includes the cardholder's name, card number and the card's expiry date.

When using a smartphone to make a contactless payment, the phone is programmed with the account information, and it's the phone emitting the RFID to the reader.

Why is it cool?

Contactless technology was invented to speed up card payments for small-value purchases. Contactless payments are capped at a certain level as a security measure – if a contactless card is lost or stolen, the amount another person could use in one transaction is limited. In some countries, this upper level of spending was raised during the COVID-19 pandemic to make it easier for people to use contactless payments.

What contactless devices are available?

The technology was originally designed to be used with bank credit or debit cards, as these are an obvious swap for cards that always required a PIN code. Today the technology has been rolled out to be used with smartphones, smart watches, key fobs and even special stickers.

This same technology is used in key fobs to open doors – specific identifying information in the chip means the reader will react only to the right key.

So what's the catch?

Some people are reluctant to use automated payments because of security fears, but if you lose your card, the technology can quickly be disabled by the bank. Others are not comfortable with each thing they buy being detailed to their account, so that not only their bank but any online sites used in the process can build up a picture of who they are and what they like to buy, and advertise to them. These issues don't exist if you buy everything with cash!

Nanotechnology

Nanotechnology is making tools and technology at the level of atoms and molecules – these are things so tiny that nothing can be built any smaller. But just because they're small doesn't mean they're not powerful and in fact, they can do some very cool, powerful stuff. The future will be filled with exciting new nanotechnologies, but there are already some exciting ones at work.

What is a nanometre?
A nanometre is a very small unit of measurement. If a centimetre was the width of the Atlantic Ocean, a nanometre would be a footstep. A human hair is about 80,000 nanometres wide!

How does it work?
Tiny clusters of atoms behave differently at the nanoscale than they do as larger lumps. This is partly because smaller particles are relatively more chemically powerful, and partly because the laws of physics act differently when you get down to the atomic level. Nanotechnologists use these different characteristics to build tools that are useful to us.

How are nanotechnologies made?
Some nanotechnology is too big to be made with chemical reactions and too small to be made physically. So, it might be made by sculpting and etching into larger materials such as silicone, or from smaller building blocks, like using molecules as Lego bricks. This can be done by directing electricity or magnetic fields at nanomaterials, so they form crystals or other structures.

The benefit is that each nanotechnology can be designed and built for very specific tasks, such as these useful ideas...

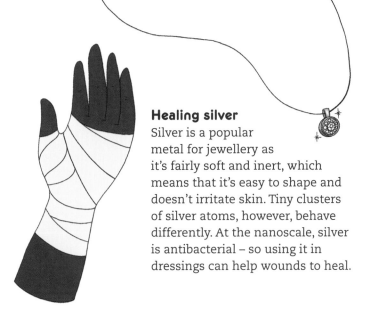

Healing silver

Silver is a popular metal for jewellery as it's fairly soft and inert, which means that it's easy to shape and doesn't irritate skin. Tiny clusters of silver atoms, however, behave differently. At the nanoscale, silver is antibacterial – so using it in dressings can help wounds to heal.

Targeting cancer

Cancerous tumours are groups of cells that are growing out of control. Traditional ways of destroying tumours use poisons that can make patients feel unwell because the poisons affect the rest of the body too.

Tiny 'nanobullets' contain special particles that bind only to cancer cells. Then, near-infra-red light is shone through the body at the nanobullets, causing them to heat up and kill the cancer cells – while leaving the rest of the body unharmed.

Cleaning up toxic waste

Toxic pollution affects so many parts of the environment – from groundwater reserves to the air and soil. Iron filings can decontaminate water through a chemical reaction, but it's expensive and inefficient. Nanotechnology can make it easier to decontaminate water. Attaching a tiny piece of the metal called palladium to each iron particle helps the molecules to work together quickly and leave behind only harmless byproducts.

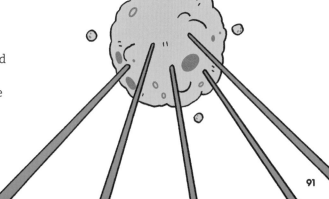

Technology for All

Through history, technology has been adapted by and for the people who use it. However, there is not a fair and equal access to useful technology across the world, or across different groups of people.

Big technological advances and new materials can be used easily and cheaply by developers – and ordinary people – to make helpful tools for all kinds of users. Adapting big technology in smaller ways can make huge differences for everyone, limited only by people's imaginations.

Waze

GPS technology helps us to know where we are in the world because our smart phones communicate with the GPS satellites that orbit the planet (see page 84). The company Waze helped to make GPS technology even more useful by sharing information between its users. Everybody using Waze as they drive shares information with other Waze users about the conditions on the roads – whether traffic is slow, if there are roadworks or blockages. In return, Waze uses that constantly updating information to offer each driver useful info such as the quickest route to their destination or the cheapest fuel station nearby.

Sugru

This inventive piece of technology is a putty-like glue that comes in lots of colours and can be moulded like modelling clay. When left for 24 hours to 'cure' in air, Sugru sets. It is then heatproof, waterproof, and flexible, and will stick to all sorts of materials, including metals, fabric, plastic, and glass.

Most importantly, it is affordable. A packet of Sugru is a technology that anyone, including children, can invent with – from fixing holes in shoes, mending broken toys, creating new toys by sticking pieces together, heatproofing mugs, making useful hooks to hold things without needing to drill any holes... The technology is useful anywhere, for anyone who can find a use for it.

Internet of Things

It's not just us who rely on the internet – many of our devices do too. The Internet of Things (IoT) is the way our devices communicate with us and with each other. Using the existing technology of the internet, the IoT allows us to do much more with smaller pieces of technology and make them even more useful.

The IoT helps people control smart technology in their homes – such as switching on the heating remotely so it's nice and warm for when you get home, but without wasting energy on an empty building. It can also help Disabled people live more independently, via equipment such as voice-controlled switches or monitors to alert carers if there's a medical emergency.

Living with the Sea

Climate change means the sea level is rising, with countries losing land and living space to the sea. The good news is that we can use innovative technology to create a liveable future in closer harmony with the rising sea level and higher tides. Countries that are low-lying are already facing these challenges with creative technological solutions.

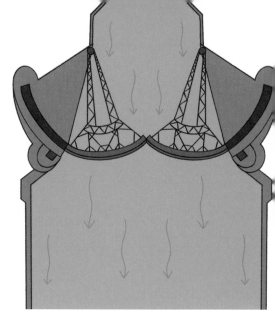

Barriers

Storm surges are not new, and many coastal and tidal areas have built reinforced banks to hold back the sea during high tides and storms. The Maldives has built a massive concrete seawall surrounding the capital, Male, which protected it during the 2004 tsunami. But such a strong structure can cause as much harm as protection. Beaches erode more easily behind seawalls, and they impact on marine life such as sea turtles, as it is harder for them to access beaches to nest on.

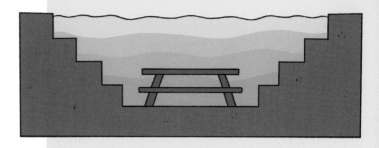

Semi-permanent barriers are better. The Maeslant storm barrier in Rotterdam, the Netherlands, is the world's largest at 20 metres high, and made of two moving barriers each as long as the Eiffel Tower is tall. If a storm surge causes the sea level to rise 3 metres the barriers close, stopping the water from entering the city.

Rooftop farms and floating farms

Is there a way of capturing rainfall in a useful way before it floods and damages living areas? Rooftop farming is one answer. Soil used in planters on top of buildings could hold 60 litres of rainwater per square metre of crops, which would otherwise add to the rising groundwater. Theses farms also cool and insulate the area from the heat produced by the building, and produce organic food, making the local area more self-sufficient.

Farms can even be located on water! Floating platforms can host homes for livestock, fruit and veg. The platforms are able to go up and down with the changing tides.

Water parks

As the sea level rises, we may have to keep building ever higher barriers. To avoid living behind protective walls, there are ways of living with the water instead. Sunken concrete parks in Rotterdam are used as basketball courts, skateboarding rinks or amphitheatres during dry weather, and when there's heavy rainfall, they change into temporary ponds as they fill up with water – saving the city from flooding. The channels to direct rainwater to the ponds were built to be large enough to carry the water and for skateboarders to use in dry weather. The public land is useful year-round, whatever the weather.

CRISPR Gene Editing

In 2020 two of the scientists that developed the CRISPR gene editing technology were awarded the Nobel Prize for chemistry. Developed in the 2010s, it is a new technology that is already treating disease and has the potential to help us fight pandemics and climate change.

How does it work?

Two scientists named Yoshizumi Ishino and Francisco Mojica found that bacteria and other microorganisms use CRISPR naturally. If a virus invades a cell, the bacteria's defence system cuts up the virus's DNA into small pieces. It then pastes some of the virus's DNA into its own so that it will always remember that virus and know to destroy it should it appear again.

Later, two more scientists – Jennifer Doudna and Emmanuelle Charpentier – realised they could use this natural phenomenon as a tool. They adapted this cut and paste technique so that we can artificially use it to recognise and edit particular parts of DNA. This could mean cutting out sections of DNA that are causing harm, or pasting in whole new helpful genes. This can be done very precisely, making the technology much safer than previous attempts at gene editing.

What does CRISPR mean?
Clustered
Regularly
Interspaced
Short
Palindromic
Repeats
. . . it's much easier to know it by the name CRISPR!

What can it do?

As soon as the technology was invented, laboratories across the world started putting it to use. It's already being trialled to restore sight to people with a rare inherited eye disease, and treat blood disorders. There are hopes it might help in agriculture too, such as making plants absorb more carbon dioxide or better resist drought, in the fight against climate change and global hunger.

Nobel Prize

In 2020 Doudna and Charpentier jointly won the Nobel Prize for their work. Although other scientists helped pave the way to the discovery, this is the first time two women have shared a Nobel Prize without a male recipient.

Technology to Feed the World

The world's population is booming and one of the biggest challenges we will face is how to grow enough food to feed everyone on the planet. By 2050 there will be 9.8 billion of us! New technology is going to be vital to help us feed the world as we battle climate change.

Space for growing food

Only 71% of the Earth is actually habitable (where humans are able to live) and around half of that habitable land is taken up with agriculture. The more people there are on Earth, the more space we need to live, but also the more food we need to produce. This leaves less space for nature and wildlife to thrive though – which we know is so important in combatting climate change and keeping the planet healthy. Technology could help us produce more with less space.

Vertical farming

Instead of using huge amounts of land for farming, we can grow plants vertically and even indoors. In cities, this could be in disused buildings, or old underground tunnels. This would reduce polluting air miles and mean food can be eaten fresher. To grow plants indoors requires the plants to be given nutrients, carbon dioxide, and light artificially. Although technology can cost more to set up, it can help us to use resources much more efficiently, with less waste.

Aeroponics

This is a way of growing plants without soil. The roots hang down and are misted with nutrient-rich moisture. It uses up to 95% less water than traditional farming, and shelves of plants can be stacked vertically, making the most of limited space.

Organic

Growing in a controlled environment means no pesticides or harmful chemicals are needed to protect plants – better for us eating the food, and for the environment because fewer dangerous chemicals can runoff into rivers and waterways.

Technology

Monitors in the growing area can ensure the plants are only misted when they need it, and LED lights above the plants enable them to photosynthesise and grow.

Climate change and unreliable water

Climate change is making weather more unpredictable, so farmers all over the world have to adapt. Drought is more common now in places such as Vietnam which traditionally used lots of water in agriculture, so technology is vital to help farmers use water efficiently.

Intelligent irrigation technology

Sensors in the earth can monitor soil moisture, rain, wind and light, and share this information with farmers. Computer software can analyse this information and suggest precise amounts of water so crops are happy but no water is wasted. Some farmers can even use devices to remotely control their irrigation systems, so plants are watered without the farmer going to the field.

Wearable Technology

As technology becomes more sophisticated and even smaller, we can integrate more of it into our daily lives while barely noticing. Wearables are accessories and clothing with built-in technology that can help us live more healthily and improve our quality of life.

Feel the music

We hear music through sound vibrations entering our ears. Wearable technology can enable us to feel music – the Soundshirt translates electrical pulses from sound vibrations to sensations we can feel over the body. Vibration motors pulsate with the intensity of the music so that different instruments are felt at different strengths in different places at different times. Technology like the Soundshirt could help deaf people experience music in a new way.

Smart ring

This simple-looking ring houses sophisticated technology that can track all sorts of rhythms and patterns in your body. When you wake up it can tell you how well you slept, monitor how much you move through the day, and your heart rate. It then gives you advice on whether you should do more exercise or go to bed earlier. By measuring your temperature, it can also be an early warning system for getting ill.

Smart rings can contain your personal information so you can use it to unlock your devices and pay for things. You could even answer a phone call by holding the ring close to your ear! With the sensors, processors, and battery power inside the ring it's still small enough to wear comfortably.

Artificial nerves

Some human reactions are automatic – such as quickly taking your hand away from a hot surface – and these can easily be taught to robots. Other reactions, such as catching a ball, are harder to perfect and learned through practice – robots learn these by repeatedly doing the same thing, and getting quicker each time. Our nerves operate on electrical impulses, and so do artificial nervous systems. These artificial systems could be made into wearable technology to learn how people move. The trained hardware would help people who have lost the ability to control their limbs, for example.

Small-Scale Energy

The world needs new ways of producing energy that don't pollute the environment in the process. We are gradually seeing more wind and solar farms taking over from fossil fuels as a way of producing energy for whole countries, but new technology is being developed to create smaller amounts of energy for more personalised use, which could become common in the future.

Backpack generator

When we walk, we move up and down, and a backpack moves up and down with us on our back. A backpack fitted with special shock absorbers could take advantage of that movement to turn it into power. The bag is allowed to slide up and down as we walk, and a pulley system uses the sliding movement to power a tiny generator that converts mechanical energy into electricity.

At the moment, this level of power could be enough to power LEDs or a watch, and is quite heavy to carry. But as the technology improves it could be made lighter and used to charge small items such as a phone while you walk.

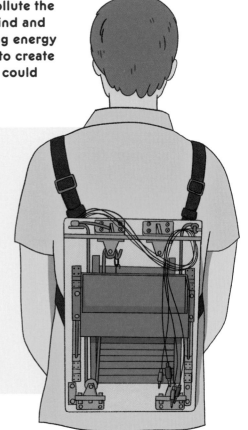

Breeze power

Using wind to power turbines is established technology – but a lot of wind is needed to turn the huge, heavy sails. Small breezes can turn lighter windmills, and developing technology aims to harvest energy from very small breezes – even ones that are created by swinging your arms while walking!

A generator can be made from two thin pieces of film each made of plastic and silver, held together in a tube. Small breeze causes the films to flutter, and as they brush against each other they cause a small electric current to travel through the silver layer to a tiny generator.

Solar panel windows

Many homes have already opted for solar panels on the roof to produce energy for their own house. But many homes do not have space or their own roof to host solar panels. New technology can turn windows into solar panels so that every home can help to produce its own green power.

A grid of nanoparticles is sandwiched between two panes of glass. When exposed to UV light, they emit tiny amounts of energy that travels along the grid to the edge of the glass, where solar cells convert it to electrical energy. The glass remains transparent so even when the windows are busy making electricity you can still look out of them.

Technology of the Future

Technology forms an important part of human history – but what about our future? Imagine how amazing the idea of a smartphone would be to someone just a hundred years ago. Some technology being developed now that might be commonplace in a hundred years sounds incredible to us now.

Growing metal

Lots of electronic technology requires rare metals to work, and forests are often cut down to mine for them, destroying the landscape and polluting the environment. To look after our planet we need to work differently, and farming metal could be an answer. Metal farms are setting up in China, Europe and Malaysia. But the new mining technology is actually plants! One tree in Borneo has bright green sap because it is rich with nickel. This metal is vital in making stainless steel, certain medical kit, and batteries used in electric cars.

Living robots

As AI develops, robots will become even more useful in our daily lives. But it could be more environmentally friendly to make robots out of living cells rather than traditional robotic parts. Living robots are actually already being developed, made from frog skin cells. When the skin cells are removed from the frog they become able to swim around using tiny hair-like structures on their surface. These tiny 'xenobots' are less than a millimetre in size, and work as a swarm to complete a task together. They could be used to do jobs in medicine and the environment. Because they are made from cells they are completely biodegradable.

Thought power

Developed to help a man with spinal cord injury who could no longer speak or use his hands to write, scientists have found a way to turn thoughts into written words. Two sensors implanted into his brain could detect electrical impulses the man set off when he imagined writing letters and words on a piece of paper. Using the technology, he can type 90 words a minute – just a little less than the average speed of someone his age typing on a smartphone.

This technology is trained to his brain so each individual would need their sensors to be set up specially for them. But perhaps in the future all of us will be able to type or communicate just by thinking.

Future Food

How will technology help us eat in the future? With an excess of cheap food available in some countries while 820 million people are undernourished, we need to make food more efficiently and distribute it more fairly.

3D printed food

Imagine if you could print out a meal specially designed for you, containing the nutrition your body needs, and just the right amount so no food is wasted. In the future 3D printers could be a standard piece of kitchen equipment. With the raw ingredients inside the printer, you could print out a tasty sandwich, or delicious edible containers filled with your choice of nutritious filling.

Dutch food futurist Chloé Rutzerveld has designed a mini vegetable garden: a 3D-printed meal of an edible breeding ground, seeds and a carbohydrate support, which grows inside its own mini greenhouse to make a delicious and healthy bite to eat.

Perhaps you could even take a quick pin-prick blood test to find out what nutrition your body most needs before planning that evening's meal, for a healthy, waste-free way of preparing food.

Laboratory meat

It takes a lot of time, space, water and food to raise a farm animal for meat. And then not all of the animal is consumed – for example there is often more demand for chicken breast than the rest of the bird. Many people choose not to eat meat for ethical reasons, too.

In the future we could be eating 'animal-free meat'. We have already worked out how to grow meat in a laboratory using animal cells, so we get the nutrition of meat without having to slaughter an animal to get it. Only one country has legalised lab-grown meat so far, and it's still more expensive than real meat, but could become affordable – and therefore available to more people. Each restaurant could have its own meat laboratory!

Allergies

Roman Emperors had official tasters to try all of their meals first in case they were poisoned. With nanotechnology coating your cutlery, in the future you could have cutlery that alerts you to any allergens in your food. If you have a peanut allergy and the cutlery sensed it in your food, it would react, alerting you, so you can avoid that food – which is definitely better than your body reacting when it's too late!

Living on Other Planets

Several countries and companies are working towards living on Mars or the Moon one day. Initially this would be creating temporary bases while we study and explore space, but perhaps in the distant future people could live there permanently. Life on Earth developed over billions of years, and on another planet we're starting from scratch – we'll need some clever technology to help.

What are the challenges?

One of the biggest challenges is that no human has ever set foot on Mars. Everything we know about it comes from telescopes and rovers, so we need to know more information about what the living conditions are actually like. We do know that there's more radiation on the Moon and Mars, which we'd need to protect ourselves from. Days on the Moon also last the equivalent of a month on Earth, so we'd have much longer in complete darkness. We'd need to find sources of food, oxygen and water – all the things humans need to live anywhere, that aren't easily available on other planets. Not only will we need to produce enough for everyone, but also deal with the resulting waste.

What might help?

NASA is developing a robot called RASSOR (Regolith Advanced Surface Systems Operation Robot) to dig regolith (space soil) and convert it to oxygen, drinkable water, and fuel sources.

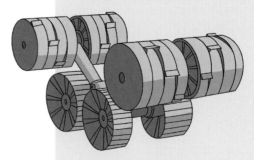

As technology develops, it often becomes smaller and more portable. This will be useful because it's difficult and expensive to send large or heavy items into space, so as time goes on we'll be able to take more useful technology into space.

Huge kites could harness energy from the strong winds on Mars to power all the tech we take up there. This would be a sustainable way to generate energy for lots of other processes.

We might be able to take some inspiration from methods behind an experimental biosphere in China. Researchers there spent 200 days without needing anything from outside the biosphere, and came up with some useful tech...

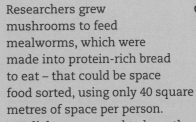

Researchers grew mushrooms to feed mealworms, which were made into protein-rich bread to eat – that could be space food sorted, using only 40 square metres of space per person. LED lights were used to keep the plants alive. As well as providing food, the plants removed carbon dioxide from the air and provided oxygen for the researchers to breathe.

Drinking water was collected by condensation and sterilised with UV light, making it safe to drink – so no need to get thirsty in space!

Water waste was treated with a bioreactor and sterilised with UV before being used to water plants. Solid waste was fermented to use as fertiliser for growing food and mushrooms – waste not, want not!

Glossary

Aeroponics – growing plants without soil.

Binary – where there are just two states of being.

Binary code – information translated into values in base-2 system.

Biomimicry – creating technology inspired by nature.

Bluetooth – a trademark for how mobile phones and other devices connect wirelessly over short distances.

Cordage – Stone Age rope made from plants.

Decimal – counting in sets of ten. Also known as 'denary'.

Digital – information given as being in one of just two possible states, such as either 'on' or 'off'.

Electronics – making technology go using electrical circuits and devices.

Frame – a single image in a video.

Gamut – the full range of colours available in a certain technology.

Generator – a machine to turn motion energy into electrical energy.

GPS – Global Positioning System – a satellite system for providing the location of a GPS receiver anywhere in the world.

Irrigation – Providing a supply of water to land to help crops grow.

Kinetic – technology that moves.

Lens – specially shaped glass to help focus light.

Nanotechnology – technology at the nano scale (smaller than the width of a human hair).

Orbit – the path a satellite takes around Earth.

Pitch – how high or low a sound is.

Prototype – a dummy version of a design, built to explain what the final version will be like and test out any problems.

Regolith – the space word for 'soil'.

Renaissance – a movement in Europe during the fourteenth to sixteenth centuries with huge breakthroughs in art, literature and science.

Resolution – the amount of information in a picture, such as dots per inch. The higher the resolution, the more information and better quality

an image is.

Sustainability – a process that is able to be maintained at a particular rate.

Synthesiser – technology to electronically put sounds together to create new sounds.

Telecommunication – communicating over great distances, further than you could speak or shout.

Turbine – a machine designed to provide continuous power. It revolves by the power of water (or other fluid), wind or steam.

Wearables – clothing and accessories with technology built in.

WiFi – a way for computers and other devices to connect to the internet wirelessly.

Technology, like art, is
a soaring exercise of the
human imagination.

Daniel Bell